Presented To

Sierra

From

On the Occasion of

Edited by Tim Dowley
Designed by Peter Wyart,
Three's Company

Worldwide coedition organized and
produced by
Angus Hudson Ltd,
Concorde House,
Grenville Place, Mill Hill,
London NW7 3SA, England
Tel: +44 20 8959 3668
Fax: +44 20 8959 3678
E-mail: coed@angushudson.com

ISBN 0-8024-3057-0

Printed in Singapore

Moody Press, a ministry of the Moody
Bible Institute, is designed for
education, evangelization, and
edification. If we may assist you in
knowing more about Christ and the
Christian life, please write to us without
obligation:

Moody Press, c/o MLM, Chicago, Illinois
60610 USA

The New BIBLE In Pictures FOR Little Eyes

KENNETH N. TAYLOR

ILLUSTRATED BY ANNABEL SPENCELEY

MOODY PRESS

CHICAGO

Introduction

Even little children can understand great truths when told to them in simple words. And when pictures are added, doubly indelible impressions are made that can last forever.

No other book has changed so many lives so remarkably as the Bible. God's Word can be a source of light to childhood's earliest pathways if carefully presented. It can be a Rock to build a life on, even when that life is very small. "Give us a child until he is five years old," some say, "and his character will be formed forever."

It is incredibly important for a child to have *direct* Bible training at the earliest possible age, in addition to experiencing the influences of a Christ-honoring home. Children can understand with simple trust the great doctrines of God and His dealings with mankind. With simple trust they can accept and always believe what hardened, older minds find difficult.

It is the hope of author and publisher that this book will be a means of establishing little minds in truths from which nothing in the years ahead can shake them, for their trust will be in the Living God and in His Son, Jesus Christ our Lord.

Kenneth Taylor

4

Contents

NEW TESTAMENT

THE OLD TESTAMENT
In Pictures
FOR
Little Eyes

God Makes the World

WHEN IT IS NIGHTTIME and the lights are out you know how dark everything gets. You can't see anything. That is how all the world once was. There were no pretty flowers; there were no trees or grass or birds. There were no children either. There was only darkness. God did not want everything to be all dark. He decided to make some people. People could not live in the darkness so God made a beautiful world full of light.

Genesis 1:2-5

Let's find out!

✦ Can you see anything at night when you go to bed and the lights are out?

✦ Did God want everything to be all dark?

Dear Lord Jesus, thank You for making light so that I can see.

14

Everyone Is Happy

*T*HIS IS THE BEAUTIFUL WORLD GOD MADE. How different it is from the cold, dark picture we looked at before! Now the world is warm and bright and pleasant. The animals are playing and everyone is happy. God has made all these things and all of them are very good but there are no people anywhere. God has not made any people. All the pretty things are here but there are no people to enjoy them, so God will make some people to live here.

Genesis 1:1

Let's find out!

✦ Can you see a lion in this picture?

✦ Can you see any people?

✦ Did God decide to make some people?

I like the beautiful world You made, Lord. Thank You for it.

God Makes Adam and Eve

*T*HESE ARE THE PEOPLE GOD MADE. Can you see them in the picture? They are behind the flowers in the middle of the picture. Can you point to them? The man's name is Adam. The lady's name is Eve. Adam and Eve did not have a mother and father. God made Adam out of dust from the ground, and then He made Eve. God made them happy and good. They love God and God loves them. In the picture you see them looking up toward God. No wonder they are so happy.

Genesis 2:7-9

Let's find out!

✦ What is the man's name?
✦ What is the lady's name?
✦ Who made Adam and Eve?

I'm happy, too, Lord Jesus.
I'm happy that You love me.

18

Adam and Eve Disobey God

ADAM AND EVE ARE NOT HAPPY NOW. Do you know why they are so sad? It is because they have been bad. They did something God told them not to do. God told them they could eat anything except the fruit from one tree. God told them not to eat that one kind but they could eat all the other kinds. The tree was so pretty and the fruit on it looked so nice that Eve wanted to eat it, but God said, "No." Then Satan, who is God's enemy, told Eve to eat it even if God said not to. Eve took the fruit and ate some of it; then she gave some to Adam and he ate it too. Now God is punishing Adam and Eve. He is sending them out of the beautiful garden and they can never come back again.

Genesis 3:8-13

Let's find out!

✦ Who are these two people?
✦ Where are they going?
✦ Why can't they stay in the garden?

Lord, sometimes I do bad things, too, and I'm sorry.

20

Cain Kills Abel

*T*HESE TWO MEN WERE ADAM AND EVE'S CHILDREN. See how big and strong they are! Once they were little children, but now they have grown up. Do you see the one with the lamb? His name is Abel. His brother's name is Cain. He is bringing some stalks of grain to give to God. Abel is giving God a lamb. God accepted Abel and his lamb, but He did not accept Cain and the grain he brought. This made Cain angry. He was so angry and jealous and mean that one day Cain said to his brother, "Let's go out and walk in the field." While they were together there in the field, Cain killed Abel. God will punish Cain for killing Abel. Cain killed his brother Abel because he was angry at God. What a terrible thing to do!

Genesis 4:8-13

Let's find out!

✦ Which of these two men is Abel?
✦ Which is Cain?
✦ Why was Cain angry?

Help me, Father God, to do the things that make You happy.

Noah Builds a Big Boat

*T*HIS MAN'S NAME IS NOAH. Can you say his name? I am glad to say that this man loves God very much. He wants to do whatever God tells him to do. He is a good man. God has told him to build a big boat. It is so big that it takes him a long, long time to build it. Can you see the big boat he is building? See how hard he and his sons are working! They are working so hard because God has told him to build the boat and he is happy to do whatever God says. Do you know why God wants Noah to have a boat? It is because God is going to send so much rain that all the ground and the houses will be covered with water, and if he does not have a boat he will die. The waters would go over his head and he would drown, but if he is in the boat he will be safe and dry. God is going to take care of Noah and his family and keep them safe and dry.

Genesis 6:13-22

Let's find out!

✦ What is this man's name?
✦ Why is he building the big boat?

*Lord, I want to be like Noah
and do just what You tell me to do.*

24

The Animals Go into the Boat

A T LAST NOAH'S BOAT IS ALL FINISHED. Can you see the boat in the picture? It is away in the back, over by the sun. See how nice the boat looks! Now it is time for Noah and his family to go into the boat. God tells Noah to take a mother and daddy lion with him into the boat. He tells him to take a mother and daddy bear too. A mother and daddy of every kind of animal are going into the boat because that is what God said. In the picture you can see all the animals going into the boat. Maybe all the other people laughed at Noah for believing that God would make it rain so hard, but Noah didn't care. He believed God and got into the boat. Then God sent the rain.

Genesis 7:6-17

Let's find out!

✦ Where are all the animals going?

✦ Who told the animals to get into the boat?

✦ Why did God want the animals in the boat?

Noah obeyed You; the animals obeyed You; help me to obey You.

It Rains for Days and Days

AFTER NOAH AND HIS FAMILY and the animals all went into the boat God sent the rain. It rained and rained, all day and all night, and for many days and nights. Down and down the rain came until all the flowers and bushes were covered up with water; soon all the houses and trees and people were covered up with the water too. Noah and his family are safe in the boat where God is taking care of them. The animals are safe too. The bird you can see in the picture is a dove that was inside the boat. Noah let it go out to see if it could find a home, but now it is coming back to the boat because of the water.

Genesis 8:8,9

Let's find out!

✦ Where are the flowers and houses?

✦ Where is Noah and his family?

✦ Where are all the other people in the world?

Thank You, Lord God, that You take good care of Your people.

28

Noah and His Family
Are Safe

*H*OW HAPPY NOAH AND HIS FAMILY ARE! They are not in the boat any more. Now at last the water has all gone away and the ground is dry again. Now Noah and his family have come out of the boat onto the dry land. They can see the grass again and the flowers and trees. Can you see what Noah is doing? He is praying to God. God is glad because Noah is praying. God says He will never again punish bad people by sending so much rain to kill them. God put a rainbow in the clouds because of His promise. Do you see the rainbow in the picture? Have you ever seen a rainbow outside your house? Whenever you see a rainbow it is God telling you that He loves you.

Genesis 8:15-22

Let's find out!

✦ What are these people doing?
✦ What is that up in the sky?

When I see a rainbow, Lord God, I will remember You always do just what You say You will do.

Proud Men Build
the Tower of Babel

*D*O YOU SEE THE HIGH BUILDING the men are making? Why are they making this high building? They want to make a high building to prove that they are very great. God does not like this. He will not let them make the building. He will make them talk so funny that they cannot understand each other. They will not be able to tell what their friends are saying. Then they will stop building the tall tower because they cannot talk to each other and cannot tell each other how to help. This building is called the Tower of Babel.

Genesis 11:1-9

Let's find out!

✦ What are the people building?
✦ Why are they building it?
✦ What will God do?

*Father God, thank You for being
the greatest and strongest one of all.*

Abraham Is God's Friend

*H*ERE IS A PICTURE OF A VERY IMPORTANT MAN. His name is Abram. Sometimes he is called Abraham. Abraham is a very good friend of God. God loves him and he loves God. God told him to take a long, long trip, to go far, far away and live there the rest of his life with his wife and his helpers and his camels and his sheep and his cows. Abraham said, "Yes," to God. He told God he would go wherever God wanted him to. Abraham loves God. He is God's friend.

Genesis 12:1-9

Let's find out!

✦ What is this man's name?
✦ What did God tell him to do?
✦ Did he do what God said?

Dear Lord, I'd like to be Your friend, too.

34

God Gives Abraham the Best

A BRAHAM IS TALKING TO HIS FRIEND whose name is Lot.
They are talking about where to live. Abraham has many
sheep and so does Lot. Sheep eat grass for their breakfast and
lunch and supper. There is not enough grass here for Abraham's
sheep and Lot's sheep too. Abraham is saying to Lot, "There isn't
enough grass here for all our sheep. Only one of us should live
here. One of us should go somewhere else to live where there is
more grass. You go where you want to live and I'll take my
sheep and live somewhere else." Lot is telling Abraham that he
wants to live where the grass is long and green and best, so his
sheep will have plenty to eat. He wants the best grass. Lot is
being selfish. He wants the best things for himself. After Lot has
taken his sheep and gone away, God will give the best land to
Abraham. Abraham isn't selfish, so God will give him the best.

Genesis 13:5-18

Let's find out!

✦ What did these two men decide ?
✦ What will God tell Abraham?

*Lord God, help me not to be selfish
and want all the good things for myself.*

God Promises Abraham a Son

ABRAHAM IS SAD. He is sad because he has no children. He needs a little boy. He talked to God about this. He asked God to give him a son. God tells Abraham to come outside with Him and look up into the sky at night and count the stars. But Abraham can't count them. There are too many to count. God says, "Abraham, I am going to give you a little boy and when he grows up he will have children, and when they grow up they will have children, and pretty soon there will be so many children that no one will be able to count them. You can't count the stars and you won't be able to count all the children and their children that I will give you." Now Abraham is happy because God will give him a little baby boy. God is glad because Abraham believed Him. Abraham knows that God will not fool him. He knows God will do just what He says.

Genesis 15:1-7

Let's find out!

✦ What is Abraham looking at?

✦ How many children did God say He would give Abraham?

O God, our Father in heaven, thank You for giving Abraham a son.

Three Men from Heaven

ABRAHAM HAS BECOME VERY OLD. See how old he is! Sarah, his wife, is old too. They are too old to have a baby. But God promised that He would give them a little boy. Three men have come to visit Abraham. Can you see them in the picture? When Abraham saw the three men he ran to meet them even though he was so old and the afternoon was so hot. Abraham knew that the three men had come to visit him from heaven. He asked them to come and eat with him and they did. They had a picnic under the trees. These men told Abraham that Sarah his wife was going to have a little baby. Sarah is laughing because she does not believe that God can give her a baby. But God will do just what He said. Soon God will give a baby boy to Abraham and Sarah. How happy they will be then! The baby's name will be Isaac.

Genesis 18:1-15

Let's find out!

✦ Where did these three men come from?
✦ What did the three men tell Abraham?

Father God, thank You for telling me again that You always do just what You promise.

God Tests Abraham's Love

GOD GAVE ABRAHAM A LITTLE BABY BOY just as He promised. Now in this picture you can see that the baby has grown to be a big boy. He is with his father Abraham and his father is very sorry. Do you know why the father is sad? I will tell you why. It is because God has told Abraham to bring Isaac here and to kill him. God wants to know if Abraham loves God best or loves his boy best. Abraham loves his boy very, very much, but of course he loves God the very best of all. Soon Abraham will obey God and take out his knife to kill his dear son. Then suddenly God will call to Abraham and say, "Stop, Abraham, stop! Don't do that. Don't hurt him. Look behind you!" Abraham will look and see a ram caught in some bushes. "Kill the ram," God will say. "Don't kill your son. I know now that you love Me." The ram will die so that Abraham's big boy can come home again with his father. Now the father is glad.

Genesis 22:1-13

Let's find out!

✦ Who did Abraham love most, God or his dear boy?

Help me, too, Lord, to love You so much that I will always obey You.

Rebekah Says She Will Be Isaac's Wife

*D*O YOU SEE THE MAN TALKING to the nice young woman? Do you know what they are talking about? The man is asking her where her father is. He wants to talk with her father. The man has come a long way. He lives with Abraham in another country. Abraham told him to go and find a wife for his son Isaac. The man asked God to help him find the right young woman. This is the woman God will give to Isaac to be his wife. The man will ask the woman and her father if she will be Isaac's wife and they will say yes. Her name is Rebekah. She will be Isaac's wife.

Genesis 24:10-26

Let's find out!

✦ What is the man saying to the woman?

✦ Who sent the man to talk to her?

✦ Will she go with him to be Isaac's wife?

Lord Jesus, thank You for helping the man find the right woman to be Isaac's wife.

Isaac Meets Rebekah

*T*HIS IS THE LADY who said she would be Isaac's wife. Her name is Rebekah. You can see Isaac running toward her. She has come on the camels for a long, long way to be his wife. She has never seen Isaac before, and Isaac has never seen Rebekah before. They are happy because God has given them to each other. Soon God will give them two babies. They will have twins, named Jacob and Esau.

Genesis 24:63-67

Let's find out!

◆ What is this lady's name?

◆ Who is running toward her?

◆ What will their children be named?

Thank You, Lord God, for giving me so many good things to be happy about.

Jacob Lies to His Father

NOW ISAAC HAS BECOME VERY OLD, and soon he will die. His two baby boys have grown up now and one of them is kneeling down in front of him. It is Jacob who is kneeling there. Jacob is not a baby now – he has become a big man and his father is very old. Jacob is telling his father a lie. His father cannot see very well because he is so old. He thinks it is his other boy who is kneeling there. He does not know that it is Jacob. The father wants to give some nice things to his other boy, and Jacob says that he is the other boy; so now the father will give the nice things to Jacob. Jacob wants nice things. He tells a lie to get them.

Genesis 27:1-25

Let's find out!

✦ What is Jacob telling his father?
✦ Why did Jacob tell a lie?
✦ Who does the father think is kneeling there?

Dear Lord, help me not to be like Jacob but to always tell the truth.

Jacob Dreams of a Ladder with Angels

NOW JACOB IS TAKING A LONG WALK to another country. His father has told him to go there to find the girl who will marry him. Jacob is tired and is lying down to sleep because it is night. He is having a dream. Have you ever had a dream? Jacob dreams that he sees stairs or a ladder that is so high that it goes right up into the sky. Angels are going up and down the ladder. Then in his dream Jacob will see God standing at the top of the ladder and telling him that many wonderful things will happen to him because God loves him.

Genesis 28:10-16

Let's find out!

✦ What is Jacob doing?
✦ Where is he going?
✦ What is his dream?

You loved Jacob, Lord Jesus;
and thank You for loving me too.

Jacob Meets Rachel and They Get Married

JACOB IS NOW A LONG, LONG WAY FROM HOME. He is in another country. He is helping a young woman whose name is Rachel. She is taking care of her father's sheep. While he is talking to her Jacob finds out that she is his cousin. She invites him to come to her house. Her father will be glad to see Jacob. He will let Jacob and Rachel get married. Jacob will live in that country with Rachel. He will not go home to his father for a long time.

Genesis 29:1-12

Let's find out!

+ What is this young woman's name?
+ Who is she talking to?

Father God, Jacob helped Rachel; and I want to be a good helper, too.

Jacob Wrestles with an Angel

JACOB IS WRESTLING WITH AN ANGEL, but they are not trying to hurt each other. Jacob wants to win so that the angel will give him many nice things. The angel touches Jacob's leg so that he cannot use it very much. The angel wants to stop but Jacob won't let him. Jacob is saying, "I will not let you go unless you bless me." Then the angel said he would give him many wonderful things. Afterward Jacob knew that the angel was God. God blessed Jacob and gave him many presents.

Genesis 32:24-30

Let's find out!

✦ Who is Jacob wrestling with?
✦ What did Jacob want?

Thank You again, Lord Jesus, for all the good things You have given me.

Esau Forgives Jacob

*G*OD TOLD JACOB TO GO with his family to another country far away. The children's grandfather lives there, and so does their uncle Esau. The children's father had stolen something from Uncle Esau, so he had been angry with their father. But in the picture you can see that Uncle Esau isn't angry anymore. How pleasant it is when people forgive each other. Have you ever been angry with someone and then forgiven them? God is pleased when we forgive.

Genesis 33:1-9

Let's find out!

✦ Are Jacob and Esau fighting?

✦ Why was Jacob afraid of Esau?

✦ Where are the children going?

Dear Lord, please help me to be kind to other people.

56

Joseph Has a Special Coat of Many Colors

*T*HIS BOY WITH THE PRETTY COAT IS JOSEPH. He is talking to his father, Jacob. Jacob loves Joseph very much. Joseph is seventeen years old and is helping to take care of the sheep. His father has given him the pretty coat as a special present because he loves him so much. The little boy is Joseph's brother. His name is Benjamin.

Genesis 37:3

Let's find out!

- ✦ What is the boy's name who has the pretty coat?
- ✦ Who gave him the coat?
- ✦ Who is the little boy?

Dear Jesus, I'm glad for the family You gave me. Thank You.

Joseph Goes to Find the Sheep and His Brothers

JOSEPH IS GOING FOR A LONG WALK to find his brothers and the sheep. His father is asking him to go and find them. Joseph is glad to help. He is telling his father, "Good-by." He will find the brothers and the sheep. But the brothers aren't nice. They don't like Joseph because their father gave Joseph the nice coat. They are angry at Joseph. They will try to hurt him. Isn't that too bad?

Genesis 37:13-27

Let's find out!

✦ Who is Joseph talking to?
✦ What does his father want Joseph to do?
✦ Will Joseph's brothers be glad to see him?

Lord, please keep me from ever wanting to hurt another boy or girl, or anyone else.

The Bad Brothers Sell Joseph

JOSEPH HAS FOUND HIS BROTHERS. But what is happening to him? Can you see him in the picture? He is the one without a shirt. Two men are taking him away. His bad brothers are selling him. Do you see the man paying money to one of the brothers? The man is buying Joseph. The cruel brothers are happy because they do not like Joseph. Now Joseph will be taken far away to another country. He can't go home to his dear father any more because his brothers have sold him and the men who bought him are taking him away. But God is watching from heaven and He will take good care of Joseph, and he will be all right.

Genesis 37:28-36

Let's find out!

✦ Which one in the picture is Joseph?

✦ Where are they taking him?

✦ Why is the man giving money to Joseph's brothers?

Father God, thank You that Joseph will be all right, because You are watching over him from heaven.

Joseph Now Works in Another Country

JOSEPH IS IN ANOTHER COUNTRY far away from his home. But God is there with him and everybody likes Joseph very much. He works hard and he always does whatever is right. The man Joseph works for likes him a lot. He has made Joseph his most important helper. In this picture you can see Joseph telling the other men what to do.

Genesis 39:1-6

Let's find out!

- ✦ Is Joseph at his own house?
- ✦ Does everybody like Joseph?
- ✦ What is Joseph doing?

Lord Jesus, thank You that You are with me when I'm at home and when I'm not at home.

God Takes Care
of Joseph in Prison

*P*OOR JOSEPH! HE IS IN JAIL. Do you see the bars on the windows so that he cannot get out? He must stay there for a long time. He has not been bad, but someone told a lie and said that he had been bad. But God is with Joseph there in jail. God is taking care of Joseph even when he cannot get out. The other men in the jail like Joseph. He tells them things that are going to happen to them. God helps Joseph know what is going to happen, and he tells the other men.

Genesis 39:20-23

Let's find out!

- ✦ Where is Joseph?
- ✦ Can he get away?
- ✦ Is Joseph telling the men what is going to happen to them?

Lord, I'm glad that You'll stay with me even when I'm having trouble.

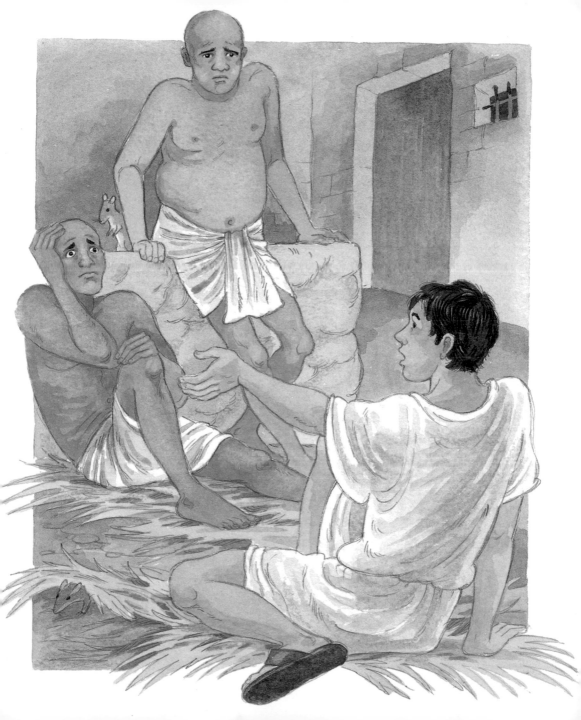

Joseph and the King's Dream

JOSEPH IS TALKING TO THE GREAT KING. Everyone is afraid of the king. He has very much money and can tell everyone else what they must do. If they do not do what he says, he will hurt them. But the king is not happy. Do you know why? It is because he had a bad dream last night. He dreamed about some cows. The cows were fat, and some other cows that were thin came and ate up the fat cows! Someone told the king that Joseph could tell about the dream and why the cows did this. Joseph was in jail but the king let him out. In this picture you can see Joseph telling the king about the dream. Joseph says that God sent the dream to the king. God wants the king to know that pretty soon there wouldn't be enough grass for the cows and they would all get very thin and hungry. God tells Joseph about the dream, and then Joseph tells the king.

Genesis 41:1-13

Let's find out!

✦ What did the king see in his bad dream?
✦ Who told Joseph what the dream meant?

Thank You, Lord, that You are a God who knows everything.

68

Everyone Must Obey Joseph

*T*HE MAN SITTING DOWN BEHIND THE HORSE is Joseph. All the people are nice to him. They like Joseph. Why do all the people like him? It is because the king has made Joseph his most important helper. Now everyone must do what Joseph says, or else the king will punish them.

Genesis 41:14-16, 38-44

Let's find out!

- ✦ Who is the man everyone is looking at?
- ✦ Do the people have to do what Joseph tells them?
- ✦ Do you know who Joseph's best friend is?

Thank You, Jesus, for being my very best friend.

Joseph Helps His Brothers

*H*ERE IS ANOTHER PICTURE OF JOSEPH. Everyone is bowing to him. The other men are his brothers. Do you remember how bad his brothers were? Do you remember that they sold him? They have not seen Joseph for a long, long time. They do not know it is Joseph they are talking to. They are afraid of this man because he is so rich and so great. They have come to buy food from him because they are hungry. These are the bad men who hurt Joseph. They sent him away when he was a young man. Joseph knows that they tried to hurt him. Do you think that Joseph will give them food? Yes, Joseph loves his brothers even though they were so bad, and he will sell them the bread they are asking him for.

Genesis 42:6-8

Let's find out!

- ✦ Who is the man sitting down?
- ✦ Who are the other men?
- ✦ Why did they come?
- ✦ Will Joseph give them bread?

Dear Lord, make me kind even to people who aren't nice to me.

Joseph Takes Care of His Brothers

JOSEPH IS TELLING THE BAD MEN that he is their brother. These men thought that Joseph was dead, but he is alive and talking to them. God has made Joseph rich and strong so that he can help his brothers and his father now that they are hungry. The brothers were bad to Joseph and made him go away, but God was with Joseph all the time and took care of him. Now Joseph is taking care of his brothers. He loves them anyway, even if they were bad. Do you know that God loves you, even when you are bad and even when He must punish you?

Genesis 45:1-15

Let's find out!

+ What is Joseph telling the men?
+ Did God take care of Joseph?
+ Will Joseph hurt his brothers because they hurt him?

Lord Jesus, I know I have done wrong things, but Your Book says You love me anyway. Thank You.

Jacob Blesses Joseph's Two Sons

*T*HIS OLD MAN IS JOSEPH'S FATHER, whose name is Jacob. Jacob is very, very old now. He knows that God will soon take him away to Heaven. Jacob is talking to Joseph, and to Joseph's two boys. He is asking God to be kind to these two boys. Jacob is blessing the two boys and praying to God about them. He is asking God to take care of them and help them.

Genesis 48:9-16

Let's find out!

✦ Who is this old man?

✦ Where is he going to go soon?

✦ Who is he talking to?

✦ What is he saying to them?

Thank You, Lord, for listening when I talk to You, just as You listened to Jacob.

The People of Israel Need Help

WHAT IS HAPPENING TO THESE PEOPLE in this picture? They are working very hard. One man is being whipped. A man wants him to work harder, and that is why he is whipping him. These people who are working so hard are God's people. They are called the people of Israel. Does God know what is happening to them? Yes, and God will help them. He will send a helper. In the next picture you will see who God's helper is going to be.

Exodus 1:7-14

Let's find out!

- ✦ What is the name of these people?
- ✦ What is happening to the man?
- ✦ Does God know about this?
- ✦ What will God do?

Father God, I'm so glad You know what is happening to me too —and that You want to help me.

78

Baby Moses

SEE THE LITTLE BABY! Why is his mother putting him in the little boat? She is putting him there because the king wants to hurt the baby. The mother is hiding him. The baby's name is Moses. When the baby Moses grows up into a big man, he will make the king of Egypt stop hurting God's people, the people of Israel. The baby will grow up and be God's helper. God is taking care of Moses by telling his mother to put him into the boat. Moses' sister will watch to see that the baby is all right.

Exodus 2:1-4

Let's find out!

- ✦ What is the baby's name?
- ✦ Why is his mother putting him into the boat?
- ✦ Will the baby be God's helper when he gets to be a big man?

Dear Lord, I want to be your helper. Please show me how to please You in everything I do.

The King's Daughter Takes Moses Home

SEE WHAT IS HAPPENING TO THE BABY MOSES! Some nice young women were walking along and saw the little basket he was lying in. The lady looking at the baby is the king's daughter. She is the king's big girl. She wants to take baby Moses home with her and take care of him. She will take the baby to her house and he will live there with her. God is taking care of baby Moses.

Exodus 2:5-10

Let's find out!

✦ Who found the little baby?
✦ Is God taking care of Moses?

Thank You, Lord Jesus, that You took good care of baby Moses —and that You want to take care of me too.

82

God Speaks to Moses from the Burning Bush

NOW THE BABY MOSES IS A BIG MAN. He is taking care of some sheep. But now God does not want Moses to take care of sheep any more. Instead He wants him to go to help God's people, the people of Israel. God wants to keep the other people from hurting His people with their whips. God is talking to Moses about this. Moses cannot see God talking to him, but he sees a bush that is on fire. The bush burns and burns, but does not burn up. Can you see the fire in the picture? God is in the burning bush and talks to Moses from there. Moses is hiding his face, for he is afraid to look at God.

Exodus 3:1-6

Let's find out!

- ✦ Where is the baby Moses now?
- ✦ Who is Moses talking to?
- ✦ Where is God in this picture?

Father God, please get me ready to do the work You want me to do when I'm grown up.

Moses and Aaron Warn the Bad King

MOSES AND HIS BROTHER AARON are talking to the king. They tell the bad king that God wants him to let the people alone and not hurt them any more. But the king laughs at Moses and Aaron. He will not stop hurting the people. He will hurt them even more. He tells Moses and Aaron to go away and stop bothering him. Then Moses and Aaron say that God will hurt the king if he doesn't stop hurting God's people. All the water in the mud puddles and in the rivers will become blood. Even what is in the glasses on the tables for lunch will become blood too. God will do this to the king to make him stop hurting God's people.

Exodus 5:6-19

Let's find out!

✦ Where is Moses?

✦ What are Moses and Aaron telling the king?

The king didn't want to please You, Lord, but I do; so help me do the things that make You happy.

The People Mark Their Doors with Blood

WHO ARE THESE PEOPLE? What are they doing? These are God's people. They are doing what God has told them to do. God said to take the blood of a lamb and put it on the sides of the doors of their houses, and on the board at the top of the door. Why did God want them to put the blood there? God is going to send an angel and in every house that does not have the blood on the door, the oldest boy will die.

Exodus 12:1-13

Let's find out!

✦ What is the man putting at the side of the door?

✦ Why is he doing that?

When I do what You tell me,
I am safe and happy.
Thank You, Lord.

The King Is Very Sorry He Hurt God's People

*I*T IS THE MIDDLE OF THE NIGHT and outside everything is all dark. In this picture everyone is crying. Do you know why? It is because the king's oldest boy has died. God's angel came and the boy died because there was no blood on the door. God said to put the blood on the door, but the king wouldn't do it. Now the king is sorry that he hurt God's people. He is sorry that he did not believe God and do what God said. Now he will tell Moses that he will stop hurting the people of Israel. He will tell Moses to take God's people out of his country so that God will not kill any more of his people.

Exodus 12:29-36

Let's find out!

+ Why is everyone so sad?
+ What will the king tell Moses to do?

Thank You, Lord, that when I do what the Bible says, then You will be with me all the time.

90

God's People Begin Their Long Journey

GOD'S PEOPLE ARE GOING ON A LONG TRIP, but they do not know where to go. Only God knows where He wants them to go. God is leading them to a good country. God has sent a big cloud that moves along in front of them. They are following the cloud. God moves the cloud and the people go wherever it goes. At night the cloud becomes fire so that the people can follow it through the darkness. That is how God tells them where to go.

Exodus 13:21, 22

Let's find out!

+ How do the people know where to go?
+ Who makes the cloud move?

Father God, when I don't know what is right to do, You want to show me. That makes me glad.

92

God Makes a Path through the Water

SEE WHAT MOSES IS DOING NOW! God has told him to stand there by the big river. How can all of God's people get across? The water is too deep, and they do not have any boats, and there is no bridge. How can they go across? Moses lifts up his hand, and see what happens! All of a sudden there is a path right through the water so that all of the people can walk through. God has told Moses to do this. God is taking care of His people so that they can get away from the bad king who wants to hurt them. God is very kind to His children. He is kind to you, too.

Exodus 14:21-31

Let's find out!

✦ What is Moses doing?

✦ What happened when Moses did this?

✦ Does God love His children?

Thank You, Lord Jesus, that You do love me very much.

The Soldiers Are Drowned

WHAT IS HAPPENING IN THIS PICTURE? Can you see Moses standing there? He is holding up his stick and now the water is coming to cover up the bad king and his soldiers. God pushed the water away so His people could walk through the sea on dry ground. They are safe now. Do you see them there behind Moses? The king chased after them with his soldiers but when he was right in the middle, God let the water come back and the soldiers drowned. You can see the water beginning to cover them up. But God's people are safe behind the cloud that God sent to help them.

Exodus 14:26-31

Let's find out!

✦ How did God's people get through the river?
✦ What is happening to the soldiers?

I'm glad You are strong and good, Lord God; You take care of Your people.

God Feeds
the People of Israel

*H*ERE ARE GOD'S PEOPLE OUT IN A FIELD. They are the people of Israel. What are they picking up from the ground? I don't think you could ever guess! They are picking up pieces of bread that God has dropped down from the skies so that they can pick it up and take it home and have it for their breakfast. There are no stores to go to, to buy food, and so God has sent the food to them. God is very kind to His children. He fed His people this way every morning, and at night he sent birds that tasted like chicken for God's people to eat for supper.

Exodus 16:2-6

Let's find out!

✦ What are these people doing?
✦ Where did the bread come from?
✦ What did God send the people for supper?

Lord, You do good things for me, too.
You know what I need.

Water Flows from the Rock

MOSES IS HITTING A ROCK WITH HIS STICK. Why is he doing this? He is doing this because God told him to. God said that if he would hit the rock with his stick all of a sudden water would come out of the dry rock and there would be a river for God's people to drink from. They were thirsty and wanted to drink, and there wasn't any water, so they started crying about it. They said mean things to Moses. Moses asked God what to do. God told him to hit the rock and water would come out. Now the people have all they want to drink.

Exodus 17:1-6

Let's find out!

✦ Were the people thirsty?
✦ What does Moses have in his hand?
✦ How did the water get there?

Thank You that You can do even the hardest things, Father God.

God Gives the Ten Commandments to Moses

*T*HIS IS ANOTHER PICTURE OF MOSES. See what he is carrying in his hands! He has two big pieces of flat stone. These stones have things written on them. God wrote on these stones and gave the stones to Moses. What does the writing say on the stones? It tells what God wants His people to do. It says to love God and obey Him. No one should ever pray to anyone but God. It says on the stones to take care of our mothers and fathers and do what they tell us to do. Another rule God gives is that we should never take anything that does not belong to us. These rules are written on the two stones. There are ten rules, so we call these rules the Ten Commandments.

Exodus 32:15-19

Let's find out!

✦ What does Moses have in his hands?

✦ What are the ten rules called?

✦ What is one of the rules on the stones?

Dear Lord, help me to always obey my mother and father.

The People Pray to a Golden Calf

OH, OH, OH! WHAT ARE THESE PEOPLE DOING? These are the people of God, but they are praying to a baby cow. Do you see the baby cow in the picture? They have made the cow out of gold and now they are praying to it. These people are disobeying God and making God very sorry. God says we must only pray to Him. These people are praying to something else. Now God must punish these people because they are so bad. Moses is very angry because the people are doing this. He is throwing down the two stones and breaking them.

Exodus 32:1-6

Let's find out!

+ What are the people praying to?
+ Who is the only One we ought to pray to?
+ What is Moses doing?

Dear Father God, I really do want to please You; help me always to obey You.

Moses Talks to God

*T*HE TENT YOU SEE IN THIS PICTURE is the place where Moses can pray to God. Moses is there talking to God. There is a big cloud at the door of the tent. The Lord is in the cloud and He will talk to Moses. You and I cannot talk to God in a cloud. But we can talk to Him right here in this room. And He sees us even though we cannot see Him.

Exodus 33:7-11

Let's find out!

✦ Where is Moses?

✦ Where is God?

✦ What is Moses doing in the tent?

I'm talking to You, Lord Jesus.
Thank You for listening to me.

The People Bring Gifts to Help Build God's House

SEE ALL THE PEOPLE COMING! See what they have in their hands! Some of them are bringing money and some of them are bringing beautiful cloth and some of them are bringing perfume. They are bringing all kinds of things. Do you know why? It is because God has told them that they could bring these things to pay for a beautiful house for God to live in. They are giving these things to God, and then some of them will help Moses build the beautiful house. The people are happy because they can give these presents to God for His house.

Exodus 35:4-29

Let's find out!

✦ What are the people bringing?

✦ Why are they bringing these presents?

Thank You, Lord, that doing what You want me to do makes us both happy.

God Watches over His House at Night

*I*T IS NIGHTTIME and some of the people of Israel are looking at the beautiful house they have made for God. Is the house on fire? No, it is not on fire, but there is a big cloud of fire there above the house. Do you know who is in the fiery cloud? It is God. God is watching over His house. He is taking care of all the people of Israel in the tents you can see in the distance. Whenever the fire began to move away, then the people of Israel took God's tent and their tents and followed the fire until it stopped. That is the way God told them where He wanted them to go when it was nighttime. In the daytime He sent a cloud for them to follow.

Exodus 40:34-38

Let's find out!

✦ Is the house burning up?

✦ Who is in the cloud?

✦ Where do all the people live?

I'm glad You are with me wherever I go, Father God, even if I can't see You.

The People Forget that God Cares for Them

*C*AN YOU SEE WHAT THESE MEN ARE CARRYING? It is a great big bunch of grapes on a pole. The grapes are so big and so heavy that the men can hardly carry them. They found the grapes far away in another country. God told them to go there. They found the grapes and brought them home for all their friends to see. God wants these people to take a long trip to that other country, where the grapes are so big, and live there. But the people are afraid to go. They think the men who live in that other country will hurt them, so they are afraid. They forget that God will take care of them.

Numbers 13:23-33

Let's find out!

✦ What are the men carrying?

✦ Where does God want His people to go?

✦ Are the people afraid to do what God says?

Because You are with me,
I don't have to be afraid. Thank You, Lord.

God Is Angry

GOD TOLD HIS PEOPLE TO LISTEN TO MOSES, but some of them said they wouldn't obey Moses any more. God is very angry with these men. God tells everyone to get away from them, because He is going to hurt them. Then all of a sudden the ground opens up and there is a big hole. They fall down into the ground, along with their houses and their friends, and everything they own. Then the earth closes up again and they are all killed.

Numbers 16:23-35

Let's find out!

✦ Did these men obey Moses?

✦ What did God do to them?

Dear Lord, I want to be a boy or girl who does just what You say.

114

The Snake of Brass

CAN YOU SEE ALL THE SNAKES IN THIS PICTURE? Do you know why they are biting the people? It is because the people have been bad again. So God has sent these poisonous snakes to bite the people, and many of the people are dying. They have come to Moses. They say, "We have been bad. Please ask God to take away the snakes." So Moses prayed for the people and the Lord told him to make a brass snake and put it on a pole. Moses took a hammer and some brass and made a snake. It isn't a real snake; it isn't alive. God told Moses that anyone who looked at the snake on the pole would get well again. The people in the picture are looking at the brass snake on the pole. Now they will be all right. But if anyone won't look, he will die.

Numbers 21:5-9

Let's find out!

- ✦ Have the people been bad again?
- ✦ What has Moses made?
- ✦ What will happen to the sick people who don't look at the snake?

Lord, thank You that You hear people when they tell You, "I'm sorry."

God Makes the Donkey Talk

A MAN IS RIDING ON A DONKEY and there is an angel standing in front of him with a long knife in his hand. The angel wants the man to stop because the man is going to do something bad and the angel doesn't want him to. The man didn't see the angel at first but the donkey did. The donkey is afraid of the angel and stops. The man is angry because the donkey stops. He hits the donkey and tells it to go on. Then the Lord makes the donkey talk, and the donkey asks the man, "Why are you hitting me?" Just then the man sees the angel standing there. The man is falling down on the ground because he is so scared. This man's name is Balaam.

Numbers 22:21-34

Let's find out!

✦ What was the man going to do?
✦ Can this donkey talk?
✦ What did it say?
✦ Why is the man falling off his donkey?

Father God, I need Your help to always want to do what is right.

Joshua Becomes the New Leader

MOSES IS SITTING DOWN ON THE ROCK. He is a very old man now. Soon he will go away to die. He will go away to live with God. He will not be with the people of Israel to take care of them any more. So now God is giving the people another leader. Now Joshua will take care of them. Joshua is talking to the people and telling them what to do. Moses tells Joshua to help the people obey God.

Numbers 27:18-23

Let's find out!

✦ Where is Moses going?

✦ Who will take care of his people now instead of Moses?

Thank You, Lord, for giving the people a new leader. Please be my leader for all my life.

Safe in the City

*T*HIS MAN IS RUNNING FAST. Do you see the other man running after him with a big knife? The first man is running into the city. He was chopping some wood with an axe and had an accident. His axe hit a man who was standing near and the man died. Then he started running away to this city and the dead man's friends chased him. You can see that he is all tired out. But now he comes to the city and the other men chasing him cannot hurt him here. God made this city so that people could run there and be safe. Now he is safe.

Numbers 35:9-32

Let's find out!

✦ Why is the man running?

✦ Where is he going?

✦ Will he be all right now that he is in the city?

✦ Can the man with the knife hurt him now?

Dear Lord, thank You for being wise and kind; You made cities of safety for the people who needed them.

Learning about God

*I*N THIS PICTURE YOU CAN SEE ONE OF GOD'S PEOPLE talking to his family. He is telling them about God. He wants them to know how good God is to him and how kind God is. He is teaching his children about God so that when they grow up they will always want to do whatever God says. He wants his children to love and obey God even now while they are still young. God always wants fathers and mothers to tell their little children about the Lord Jesus. That is why I am reading these good stories from the Bible to you—so that you will know more about God.

Deuteronomy 6:7-14

Let's find out!

✦ What is the man telling his family?

✦ When you become grown up, what will you tell your children?

I want to love and obey You, Lord Jesus, even while I'm still not very old.

Bringing Gifts to God

*T*HESE PEOPLE ARE BRINGING GIFTS TO GOD. They want to give them to God because they are so glad God has been kind to them. The grapes are from their own gardens. Do you see the baskets of grapes? See how many there are! They are taking the first of these grapes and are bringing them to God's house for the priest or minister to use. They will give some to poor people who do not have enough to eat.

Deuteronomy 26:1-11

Let's find out!

+ What is in the basket?
+ Where is the man taking them?
+ Why does he want to give the grapes to God?

Father God, thank You that the money I give to You at Sunday School and church will help other people.

Moses Sees
the Promised Land

MOSES IS ON A MOUNTAIN. He is standing on the top of the mountain. He is looking over to the country that God will give to the people of Israel. Moses cannot go there because once he did not obey God. God said that he would have to be punished by not getting to go to the nice country. But God will let him see the Promised Land. God is showing it to him now. God told Moses to come up to this mountain so that he could look at it. In a little while Moses will die and God Himself will put Moses' body into the ground. But Moses will go to live with God while his body is there in the ground.

Deuteronomy 34:1-12

Let's find out!

+ Will Moses go to the country where he is looking?

+ What is going to happen to Moses?

Thank You, Lord God, for wanting mothers and fathers and boys and girls to live in heaven with You.

128

Joshua's Men Are Helped by a Lady

IT IS NIGHT OUTSIDE. A man is climbing down from a high window. Soon another man will come down too. A woman is helping them. These two men do not live here. They live in another country. They live with Joshua and God's people. God told them to come here and see this city. The name of the city is Jericho. When these two men came to the city, the people who lived there tried to catch them, but the woman is helping them get away. God will be kind to her because she is helping these two men.

Joshua 2:1-15

Let's find out!

+ Do these two men live here?
+ What did the people try to do to them?
+ Who helped them get away?

The kind lady helped Your people, Lord. Make me a good helper, too.

God Makes a Way Across the River

GOD IS DOING A WONDERFUL THING for His people. He wants them to go across the river to the land He said He would give them. There is no bridge for them to go across, and no boat, and the water is too deep to wade. But God makes a way for them to go across. See how the water is standing up like a wall! Now there is a path through the bottom of the river for the people to walk on. The ground is dry beneath their feet. Look at the priests walking ahead of the people of Israel and carrying God's Ark. God is making the water stand up instead of getting the people all wet.

Joshua 3:13-17

Let's find out!

◆ How did the people get across the river?

◆ What is happening to the water?

◆ Who fixed the river so the people could walk across the bottom of it?

Father God, thank You for being strong enough to do anything I need.

132

The Walls Fall Down

*G*OD'S PEOPLE ARE WALKING AROUND the big city called Jericho. God has told His people to walk around it every day. They have already walked around it once yesterday. They have walked around it once every day this week. Today God told them to walk around it seven times instead of once. Now the people are yelling very loudly and the priests are blowing their trumpets. The high walls are falling down, and now all of God's people can walk right into the city. The people in the city built high walls to keep them out, but God is knocking down the walls. This is the city where the woman lives who helped the two men climb down the wall. The people of Israel do not hurt her when they go into the city because she was kind to them.

Joshua 6:1-20

Let's find out!

- ✦ What is happening to the walls?
- ✦ Tell what the people did each day.
- ✦ How many times did they walk around it on the seventh day?

Thank You, Lord Jesus, that nothing is too hard for You.

God Keeps the Sun from Setting

*D*O YOU KNOW WHO THIS MAN IS? He is Joshua, the leader of God's people. God's people are having a great fight with some other people. In the picture you can see all the men fighting. The sun is beginning to go down. It will be dark. Joshua and God's people will not be able to see to fight. In this picture Joshua is talking to God about the sun. He is asking God to keep the sun from going down. He wants it to stay where it is so that it won't get dark for a long time. God listened to Joshua's prayer and answered it. It will not get dark as soon as usual because God is keeping the sun up there in the sky. How powerful our God is.

Joshua 10:6-15

Let's find out!

✦ Did Joshua want it to become dark?

✦ What did Joshua ask God to do with the sun?

Thank You for making the sun and moon, and for making them obey You.

Gideon Chooses His Helpers

WHY ARE THE MEN DRINKING WATER? Some of them are putting their mouths into the water and drinking like dogs. Others are putting the water into their hands. They will drink out of their hands. Can you see which ones are drinking from their hands? God told Gideon to tell the men to drink the water. He told Gideon to choose the men who drink out of their hands. Gideon will take these men with him to fight with the people who don't like God. He will send all the other men home. God only wants a few men to go. There will not be enough men, so God will help them. God will help them and they will win.

Judges 7:2-7

Let's find out!

+ Did God want Gideon to take lots and lots of people with him to fight?
+ What are the men doing?
+ Which ones did Gideon ask to go with him?

Dear Lord, I want to be like Gideon and do what You tell me to do.

Samson Carries the City Doors Away

*T*HIS IS A PICTURE OF SAMSON. Samson is the strongest man who ever lived. He is strong because God made him that way and helped him. God said that as long as he did not cut his hair he would be strong. Do you see his long hair? Here is a picture of Samson and some heavy doors. They are the doors to keep people from going in and out of the walls of that city he is looking at. The doors are shut, and Samson wants to go out. He does not have the key, so he goes out anyway and just takes the doors along with him! What a strong man Samson is!

Judges 16:3

Let's find out!

+ What is the man's name?
+ Did he have the keys to the door?
+ How did he get out?

I'm not strong like Samson, Lord,
but You made me able to do many things.
Thank You.

Samson Pulls Down the House

*T*HE STRONG MAN, SAMSON, has chains on his feet. Can you see the chains? How did they get there? I will tell you. One night when he was asleep some men cut off his long hair. Then Samson wasn't strong any more. The men put chains on him and made him blind by hurting his eyes. But now Samson's hair has grown long again and he is stronger. He asked the men to let him stand by the two posts that held up the house. He is pulling the house down and Samson and the people will all die.

Judges 16:18-30

Let's find out!

+ What did the men do to Samson's hair?
+ How did Samson get the chains on his feet?
+ What happened after Samson's hair grew out again?

Thank You, Lord, that You love us even when You let bad things happen to us.

Ruth Goes Away with Her Mother

*T*HIS DEAR MOTHER IS GOING AWAY. Now she will live somewhere else in another country far away. She is saying good-by to Ruth. But Ruth doesn't want her to go all by herself. Ruth wants to go with her and take care of her. Ruth is kind and good.

Ruth 1:8-18

Let's find out!

+ Is Ruth kind and good?
+ Will she go away from the mother?
+ Does Ruth want to take care of her?

Please, Lord, make me kind and good to other boys and girls.

144

Ruth Works Hard

*T*HIS IS A PICTURE OF RUTH. Do you remember how kind she was to her mother? Now she is working hard to get food for both of them to eat. Do you see the wheat in Ruth's hands? She will use it to make bread to eat.

Ruth 2:5-17

Let's find out!

+ Who is this lady?
+ What does she have in her hands?
+ What will she do with it?

Ruth was such a good worker, Father God. Make me a good worker, too.

Hannah Prays for a Baby

*H*ANNAH IS PRAYING. She is praying because she does not have a baby, and she wants one very badly. She and her husband have come to God's house to pray and to give gifts to God. The minister sees her praying. He tells her that God will answer her prayer. God will send her a little baby because of her prayer.

1 Samuel 1:9-19

Let's find out!

✦ Why was Hannah praying?
✦ What does the minister tell her?

I know You listen when I pray, Lord. Thank You.

God Answers Hannah's Prayer

GOD GAVE HANNAH A LITTLE BABY BOY. You can see him in the picture. The little boy's name is Samuel. Samuel was a tiny baby but he grew and grew and now he is not a baby any more. Hannah wants to give her little boy to God. She has brought him to God's house to be a helper to the minister whose name is Eli. The little boy Samuel is talking to Eli. Samuel's mother will go home now and Samuel will not see her very much. He will live with Eli and be God's helper.

1 Samuel 2:18, 19

Let's find out!

✦ What is this little boy's name?

✦ Who will Samuel live with now?

✦ What will he do?

Thank You for giving Hannah her little boy, Father God; I thank You for giving me good things, too.

Samuel Hears God Talking to Him

SAMUEL IS GROWING TALLER. He has been asleep. Now he is awake. He is listening to someone talking. He hears someone calling, "Samuel! Samuel!" He thinks that Eli is calling him from the next room.
He runs quickly to Eli and says, "Here I am, you called me." But Eli says, "No, I didn't call you." "Who called me, then?" Samuel wants to know. Eli tells him that God was talking to him. Samuel will listen to what God says, and do it.

1 Samuel 3:1-10

Let's find out!

✦ Was Eli calling Samuel?
✦ Who was calling him?
✦ What is Samuel going to do?

Dear Lord, please make me quick to obey You, just like Samuel.

The Messenger Tells Eli Some Bad News

*E*LI IS SITTING ON A ROCK while a man is telling him what has happened. God's people have been fighting with some bad men called the Philistines. The man is telling Eli that God's people are all running away, and that Eli's two sons have been killed. Now Eli is very sad. The man tells him that God has let the Philistines win the fight and capture the Ark. When Eli hears this he falls off the rock he is sitting on, and he is hurt so badly that he dies.

1 Samuel 4:5-18

Let's find out!

+ What is the man telling Eli?
+ Is he telling him happy things?
+ What happened to Eli when he heard about it?

Thank You again that You love me, Lord, even when sad things happen.

154

Saul Is Chosen to Be King

THE LITTLE BOY SAMUEL IS NOW AN OLD, OLD MAN. Samuel is pouring oil on the head of a young man whose name is Saul. God has chosen Saul to be king over His people Israel. See how strong Saul is! See how he is kneeling there in front of Samuel! Samuel is pouring some oil on Saul's head because Saul is going to be the king. It looks like he will make a good king for all of God's people to obey. But do you know something that is very sad? I will tell you what it is. Saul's heart has sin in it. That means that Saul will do wrong things.

1 Samuel 9:15-27

Let's find out!

✦ What is the name of the young man?
✦ Why is Samuel pouring oil on his head?

Lord, please help the president of our country to be a good leader.

David the Shepherd

THIS FINE YOUNG MAN IS DAVID. He takes care of sheep. When a lion came to catch David's sheep, David killed the lion. Can you see the lion lying there under his knee? David is strong and good and God is going to let him be the king over His people. God wants Samuel to pour oil on David's head now, so that David will know that he is going to be the king.

1 Samuel 16:1-13

Let's find out!

◆ What is the name of this young man?

◆ Does he take care of sheep?

◆ Will he become king?

Thank You, Father God, that You have some special work for me to do when I grow up.

158

David Sings to God

*T*HIS IS A PICTURE OF DAVID. In the Bible there are many songs that David wrote and played on his harp. In this picture you can see him playing and singing. The music is very pretty and the words are nice because they tell how much he loves God. Some of the words he wrote are:

"The Lord is my shepherd,
I have everything I need.
He lets me rest in green meadows.
He leads me beside peaceful streams."

Psalm 23

Let's find out!

- ✦ What is the name of this young man?
- ✦ What is he doing?
- ✦ Where are some of his songs written down?

Thank You, Lord Jesus, for watching over me like a good shepherd.

David Kills Goliath

A GIANT HAS COME TO FIGHT against God's people. The giant's name is Goliath. All the men of Israel have run away from him. They are afraid to fight him because he is so big but David is not afraid. David knows that God will help him. David does not have a gun but he has a slingshot. Do you see it in his hand? He takes some stones and uses his slingshot to throw a stone at the giant. The stone hits the giant in the head and the great Goliath falls over dead.

1 Samuel 17:38-50

Let's find out!

✦ What is the giant's name?

✦ What did David hit him with?

✦ Why were all the other people afraid of Goliath?

I don't fight giants, Lord, but some other things are hard for me to do. Please help me.

David and Jonathan

DAVID AND JONATHAN ARE TALKING together. They are good friends and like to talk to each other. Jonathan is King Saul's son. He is a prince. But Jonathan will never be the king because God has told David to be king. Does this make Jonathan sad and angry? No, Jonathan loves David and he is glad that David is going to be the king. Do you see David and Jonathan talking together in the picture?

1 Samuel 20:4-17

Let's find out!

✦ What are the names of these two men?

✦ What is the name of the one who is going to be the king?

Lord Jesus, I thank You for my good friends.

David Finds Saul Asleep

*T*HE MAN WHO IS ASLEEP IS KING SAUL. He has been chasing David. He wants to catch him so that he can hurt him and kill him. Saul does not like David. He knows that God is going to make David king instead of him. Saul wants to keep on being king but God won't let him. David and a friend with a spear find King Saul sleeping. David's friend wants to kill King Saul with the sharp spear. But David is good and he won't let his friend hurt King Saul. David knows God would not like this. David only wants to do whatever God tells him. David obeys God.

1 Samuel 26:5-25

Let's find out!

+ Can you see King Saul?
+ What is he doing?
+ Can you see David in the picture?
+ What is he doing?

Help me, Lord, to be just like David and do what the Bible tells me.

166

King David

*D*AVID IS THE NEW KING. The old man is Samuel. He is pouring oil on David's head. He is doing this to make David king because that is what God said. Now everyone must obey King David. A long time before this God told David that some day he would be king, and now he is.

2 Samuel 2:1-4

Let's find out!

✦ Who is the new king?

✦ What is the old man, Samuel, doing to David?

I'm so glad You never lie, Father God;
You always do just what You say You will do.

The Golden Ark
Is Brought Home

DAVID IS BRINGING HOME THE ARK. If anyone looked into the Ark he would die. The Ark belongs to God. David is happy that the Ark is coming. He is walking along in front of it playing on his harp. Everyone is happy because God is coming to live with them.

2 Samuel 6:12-19

Let's find out!

- ✦ Is David happy?
- ✦ What happens to people who open the golden box?

Lord God, thank You that You live here with me in our home all the time!

God Sends Nathan to David

*T*HE MAN WITH THE CROWN on his head is King David. God has sent Nathan the prophet to talk to him. See how he is pointing his finger at King David and how David is afraid. David has done a very bad thing and God saw him do it. God sent Nathan the prophet to tell David that God is going to punish him. David is sorry that he has been so bad and asks God to forgive him. God forgives David but he will punish him very much for the bad thing he has done.

2 Samuel 12: 1–10

Let's find out!

✦ Which of these men is King David?
✦ Has David been good or bad?
✦ Who sent the other man to talk to King David?
✦ Did God punish David for being bad?

I do wrong things sometimes, too, Lord, and then I need You to forgive me.

172

Absalom Gets Caught

THIS MAN WHO IS GETTING CAUGHT UP there in the tree is Absalom. Absalom is David's son. He is a prince because his father is the king. Absalom doesn't want his father to be king any more because he wants to be king instead. God does not like this. God wants David to still be king. Now look at Absalom. He is caught in the tree. His mule is running away. He has been riding on the mule but now he will hang there by his hair because it has gotten all tangled up in the tree and he cannot get down. Soon some men will come who do not like Absalom. He will not be able to get away from them and they will kill him. Now Absalom cannot be the king. God does not want him to be king.

2 Samuel 18: 9–18

Let's find out!

+ What is happening to Absalom?
+ Can he be king?
+ Did God want Absalom to be king?

Absalom didn't care what You wanted, Lord Jesus, but I care. Help me to please You.

Solomon Is a Wise King

KING SOLOMON IS TELLING TWO WOMEN what to do. They have come to ask him what to do with the little baby they are holding. Each of them says that the baby is hers. One of them is telling a lie. Which one is it? God tells Solomon how to find out. He says to cut the baby in half and give half of it to each of the women. Then the baby's mother said, "No! No! Let the other woman have the baby. Don't cut it in half!" Then Solomon knew the woman who didn't want the baby hurt must be the baby's mother. Solomon gave the baby to his mother. God made Solomon very wise.

1 Kings 3:16-28

Let's find out!

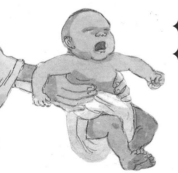

+ Did the baby's mother want him to be hurt?
+ Who made Solomon wise?

O Lord, thank You that You are so wise.
Help me to become wise, too.

Solomon Builds a New House for God

KING SOLOMON BUILT THIS HUGE HOUSE. Do you know whom he made it for? It is God's house. It took a long time to build it because it is so nice. Many men have cut down trees and made them into boards and other men cut big rocks and worked very hard. Solomon is glad because he could make this beautiful house for God to live in.

1 Kings 6:11-14

Let's find out!

✦ Whose house is this?

✦ Is Solomon glad?

Thank You that Solomon built this home for You to live in. And thank You for living in my heart.

Solomon Gives Thanks

SOLOMON IS STANDING in front of God's house. See all of the people who have come to have a big party because they are so glad that God's house has been built! Now it is all finished and Solomon is praying. He is standing there with his hands raised before Heaven talking to God. He is thanking God for being so kind to him and to his people and to his father David. He is asking God to take care of them and help them all the time. God is listening. God says He will take care of the people as long as they do what He tells them.

1 Kings 8:22-29

Let's find out!

✦ Why have all the people come to God's house?
✦ What is Solomon doing?
✦ Is God listening?
✦ What does God say?

You listened to King Solomon, Father God.
Thank You for listening to me too.

180

Solomon Prays to an Idol

WHAT A SAD THING IS HAPPENING! Solomon the great king God loves is bad. He is praying to someone else. He is praying to that thing standing there. A man made it and it is not even alive. It is called an idol. Solomon is praying to it. It cannot hear Solomon's prayer because it is not alive. God in heaven is watching Solomon. He is very angry about this. God says that now Solomon must be punished. Poor Solomon! Why did he do such a wrong thing? I wish he had remembered to love God and had never prayed to the idol.

1 Kings 11:1-10

Let's find out!

✦ Is Solomon praying to God?

✦ Where is God?

✦ Will God punish Solomon?

Lord, keep me from being foolish and forgetting You, as this foolish king did.

The Birds Bring Food to Elijah

*T*HIS MAN IS ELIJAH. He is a great friend of God's. Elijah is good but other people tried to hurt him. Elijah asked God to stop it from raining for a long, long time. God listened to Elijah and stopped all the rain. Now the king is angry at Elijah for asking God to do this. Elijah is afraid of the king and runs away and is sitting here by a little river. There is no food here for him and no stores where he can buy it so God is sending him some. The birds are bringing food to him. God is taking care of his friend Elijah.

1 Kings 17:1-7

Let's find out!

+ What did Elijah ask God to do to the rain?
+ Why is he hiding?
+ How is Elijah getting food?

Father God, You always have ways to give us what we need. Thank You.

The Little Boy Is Brought to Life

*T*HIS LITTLE BOY WAS OUT PLAYING. Then he began to feel sick. After a while his mother put him into his bed but he didn't get any better. Then the little boy died. His mother asks Elijah to make him alive again. Elijah could not make the little boy alive unless God told him to. Elijah asks God to make the little boy alive and all better again. In this picture you can see what happened when Elijah prayed. The little boy is all right and Elijah is giving him to his happy mother.

1 Kings 17:17-24

Let's find out!

✦ What happened to the little boy?
✦ Who did the boy's mother ask to help?
✦ What is happening in the picture?

You are a great God, Lord. You are able to do special things whenever You want to.

Elijah's Fire Is Lit by God

*I*N THIS PICTURE YOU CAN SEE ELIJAH praying to God. He is asking God to send fire from Heaven to light the big sticks he has piled on the stones. Do you see the stones and the sticks? Suddenly a great flame of fire comes sweeping down from the sky. God sent the fire because Elijah asked him to. The fire is burning the sticks. How frightened and surprised God's enemies are as they watch. They did not know that God would answer Elijah's prayer. But Elijah is not surprised. He knew that God would hear him. Now all the people know that the Lord is the only God.

1 Kings 18:20-39

Let's find out!

+ Where is the fire coming from?
+ Did God hear Elijah's prayer?

I'm happy that You do such wonderful things, Father God, and that whatever You do is right.

The Chariot Takes Elijah to Heaven

*E*LIJAH IS GOING UP TO HEAVEN. His friend Elisha is watching on the ground. They were walking along together when all of a sudden this chariot of fire came down from heaven and took Elijah up to God. Elisha sees him go. He is picking up Elijah's coat. Now Elisha will not be able to talk to Elijah any more but he can still talk to God. God is with Elisha and talks to him and makes him strong.

2 Kings 2:1-14

Let's find out!

✦ Who is in the fiery chariot?

✦ Where is he going?

✦ What is the name of the man who is picking up the coat?

Lord, I'm glad that I can talk to You too, like Elisha did after Elijah had been taken up to heaven.

The Oil Jar Never Gets Empty

*D*O YOU SEE THIS LADY and her two boys? She must pay some money to a man tomorrow, or the man will take her two boys away from her. He will make them come and live in his house and work hard. Elisha tells her to get all the jars and pans that she can find. He tells her to take the little jar of oil she has in her hand and pour it out into the other jars. She keeps pouring it out but her little jar never gets empty! The oil in it fills all the big jars. See how many big jars she has already filled up. She will sell the oil and get enough money to pay the man so that she can keep her children. God never let the little jar get empty.

2 Kings 4:1-7

Let's find out!

+ Why was the lady sad?
+ What did Elisha tell her to do?
+ Why doesn't the little jar get empty?

You gave the mother what she needed, Lord God; thank You for giving me all that I need.

The Sick Man Looks for Elisha

*T*HIS LADY IS WAVING GOOD-BY TO HER HUSBAND. He is going away. He is sick. The girl sitting there told him about God and about God's friend Elisha. The girl said that Elisha could make the sick man well again. He is going away to find Elisha and to ask Elisha to make him well. Elisha will ask God to help and then the man will be all well again. It was nice for the little girl to tell the man and his wife about God. The man did not know about God until the little girl told him.

2 Kings 5:1-14

Let's find out!

✦ What did the little girl tell the man and his wife?

✦ Where is the man going?

Father God, please help us to tell others about You, as the little girl did.

194

The Man Is Made Well

*T*HE MAN IN THE RED ROBE is God's helper, Elisha. The man with the gold helmet had been sick. He asked Elisha to make him well again. Elisha told him to go down to the Jordan River and wash in it seven times and then he would be well. At first the man didn't want to do this. He thought it was a funny way to get well. But soon he went to the river. One, two, three, four, five, six, seven times he washed himself in the river and then he was well again. He is bringing presents for Elisha, to pay for making him well, but Elisha says, "No." Elisha doesn't want his money. Elisha is glad because now the man will only pray to our God, and not to any idol.

2 Kings 5:9-16

Let's find out!

+ Had the man with the gold helmet been sick?
+ What does Elisha tell him to do?
+ Does Elisha want his money and gifts?

Thank You, Lord, for making the man well —and especially that he found out about You.

Elisha Watches the Angels

*E*lISHA IS SITTING ON TOP OF HIS HOUSE. He is watching some angels up in the sky. They have come to help him and the boy who is there with him. Some bad people want to hurt Elisha so God sends these helpers. They won't let anybody hurt Elisha and his friend.

2 Kings 6:13-17

Let's find out!

✦ What is happening in this picture?

✦ Can we always see the angels?

✦ Are there any angels here in this room?

Thank You for the angels that You send to help me, even if I can't see them.

The Little Boy Is King

*T*HIS LITTLE BOY IS SEVEN YEARS OLD but he is already the king over God's people. God has said that everyone must obey him. He has helpers so that he will know what to do. The little boy's name is Jehoash and he loves God very much. The people are happy because he is their king. When he grows older he will notice that God's house needs to be fixed up and he will fix it. I am sorry to say that when he becomes a big man he won't love God so much. Then he will pray to idols. What a sad thing to happen! When you get big I hope that you will only love God and pray to Him. The little boy in the picture will be very sad after he forgets about God.

2 Kings 11:1-12

Let's find out!

- ✦ How old is the little king?
- ✦ Will he still love God when he grows up?
- ✦ How old are you?
- ✦ Do you want to love God when you grow up?

Lord Jesus, I love You and when I am grown up I want to keep on loving You with all my heart.

Hezekiah Asks God to Help Him

KING HEZEKIAH IS CRYING OUT TO GOD for help. He got a letter from a man who said that he was going to bring a lot of soldiers to catch him. King Hezekiah is very sad and doesn't know what to do. So he comes to God's house to pray and to ask God about it. He is saying, "O Lord, save me and my people! Show everyone how strong You are and that You are our God." God hears King Hezekiah praying. He will send a man soon to tell him that God will help. God will answer Hezekiah's prayer and take care of him.

2 Kings 19:1-20

Let's find out!

+ Why is the king sad?
+ Who is he talking to?
+ Does God hear King Hezekiah?

Dear Lord, thank You that when we don't know what to do, You know and You will tell us.

Josiah Reads God's Book

*T*HE MAN SITTING ON THE CHAIR is another of God's kings. His name is Josiah. He became king when he was just a little boy eight years old. Now he is grown up into a big man. See how surprised he looks! Someone is showing him a Book that he has found in God's house. It is part of the Bible. The king has never seen the Bible before and did not know what God wanted. Now he will begin to do whatever God says because he has found God's Book and can read it.

2 Chronicles 34:18-28

Let's find out!

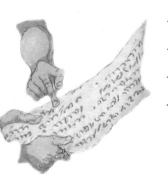

- ✦ Why is the king surprised?
- ✦ Where did the man find God's Book?
- ✦ Do you have a Book that tells what God says?
- ✦ What is the name of the Book?

Thank You, Father God, that we have Your Book, the Bible, in our house.

The Men Are Sorry for Doing Wrong

*T*HESE PEOPLE ARE ALL CRYING because they have done such bad things. The man who is talking to them is Ezra. He is one of God's friends so he knows what God wants them to do. Do you know what they have done? These men have married women who do not know about God. These women want God's people to pray to sticks and stones instead of to God. This is very wrong. Ezra tells the men how bad it is for them to marry someone who doesn't love God. Now these men are sorry for what they have done. We should never marry anybody who does not love the Lord Jesus.

Ezra 10:1-12

Let's find out!

✦ What did these men do?

✦ Can you guess what Ezra is reading to the men?

Thank You, Father God, that Your Book, the Bible, tells us how to please You.

Whatever Happens, Job Still Loves God

*T*HE MAN IN THE PICTURE, who doesn't have any shirt on, is named Job. He was very rich. He had many sheep and cows. Then he lost all of his money and animals. Now Job is very sick and sad. Satan has taken away all of his cows and camels and all of his boys and girls so that he doesn't have anything left. Now he is very, very poor. Job is sorry but he does not blame God. He says, "God, You are good and I love You no matter what happens to me."

Job 1:1-22

Let's find out!

- ✦ What is this man's name?
- ✦ What happened to all of his cows?
- ✦ Does Job still love God?

I'm glad, Lord, that You are with me and that You love me even when I have big troubles.

Job Is Now Well and Happy Again

*H*AVE YOU SEEN THIS MAN BEFORE? Yes, this is Job, the man who became so poor and sick and now he is all right again. God has given him more than he had before. He has more cows and more sheep and more money. Job knows God is good. Job loves God and God loves Job. Do you love God like Job did? Will you do what God says even if God lets you become sick or hurt? I hope you will always love God more and more because God loves you so much.

Job 42:10-17

Let's find out!

✦ What is the name of this man?
✦ Has God made him rich again?

Help me, Lord, to love You when I have lots of toys and when I don't.

Isaiah the Prophet

*T*HIS IS A MAN WHOSE NAME IS ISAIAH. God sent him to tell the people what they should do. He is called a prophet. Can you say "prophet"? The people are bad and God sends him to tell them to stop being bad. He says that if they don't, God will hurt their country, and wreck their cities, and burn up their houses. God is sorry when His people sin and do wrong things. God sends Isaiah to help them stop doing what is bad.

Isaiah 1

Let's find out!

+ Tell about something you have done that is wrong.

+ Tell Jesus if you are sorry, and ask Him to forgive you.

Lord Jesus, help me to stop doing things that are wrong.

God Will Make Everything Happy

*L*OOK AT THE LITTLE CHILD. Do you see all the animals that are with him? He is touching the cow. A big lion is standing quietly beside him. The lion does not hurt him. Do you see the little lamb, and the black wolf behind the lamb? The wolf does not eat the lamb or hurt it. Some day God will make everything happy. He will make cats and dogs like each other instead of chasing each other. The children will not quarrel and nothing will hurt them. God will make everything want to be kind and gentle.

Isaiah 11:1-10

Let's find out!

- ✦ Will the lion hurt the little child?
- ✦ What is God going to do some day to the cats and dogs?

What a happy time it will be, Father God, when Jesus comes back! He will make all the wrong things right.

Jeremiah Is Tied Up

*T*HIS MAN IS JEREMIAH. Can you say "Jeremiah"? He is one of God's friends. God has sent him to tell the people to be good. The people do not like Jeremiah to tell them this. They want to be bad so they have tied Jeremiah's hands together. They will put him in a room and lock the door so Jeremiah cannot get away. He must sit there all day. People go by laughing at him and making fun of him. Poor Jeremiah! But God is with him and God will punish the people who did this to His friend.

Jeremiah 32:1-5

Let's find out!

+ What has happened to Jeremiah's hands?
+ Is Jeremiah God's friend?
+ Will God be with Jeremiah?

Lord, some of Your people are in trouble right now just because they are doing what is right. Please help them know that You are with them.

God Speaks to Jeremiah

*H*ERE IS ANOTHER PICTURE OF JEREMIAH. Do you remember seeing him in the last picture? Jeremiah is talking to another man who is writing down all the things that Jeremiah tells him to. God is talking to Jeremiah and telling him what to say to the man, and the man is writing it down. He is writing down what God says. He is writing part of the Bible. The Bible is what God says and wants us to know. When the man has finished writing the Book he will read it to all the people, so they will know what God wants them to do.

Jeremiah 36:1-4

Let's find out!

✦ What is Jeremiah doing?

✦ Who is telling Jeremiah what to say?

✦ What is the man doing who is sitting down?

Thank You that we too can know what pleases You, because we have Your Book, the Bible.

The King Is Angry

*I*N THE LAST PICTURE DO YOU REMEMBER how Jeremiah listened to God and told a man what to write? When it was all written down, God said to take it to the king so he would know what God said. The king read some of it. It said for him to be good and to stop doing bad things. The king is very angry. He does not want to obey God. Oh, oh, do you see what a terrible thing he is doing? He is throwing God's letter into the fire. He is burning it up. He does not want to have God's letter. Oh, how much God will have to punish this king because he will not listen to God or obey Him!

Jeremiah 36:19-24

Let's find out!

+ Who is this man?
+ What is he doing?
+ What will happen to the king?

Lord, I'm sorry the king did not care what You said, but I care; help me to do what You tell me in Your Book.

God's People Are Taken Away

*H*ERE IS A SAD PICTURE. It is a picture of God's people being taken away to another country. They are going away from their homes. They want to go home but they can't. The people who are taking them away do not like them and will hurt them and kill some of them. See how sorry the people are! Do you know why this has happened? It is because they are God's people but they have done bad things and God is punishing them. They have prayed to sticks and rocks and the sun instead of praying to God. Instead of spanking them, God takes them away to another country where they don't want to go. In the picture you can see them going away.

Jeremiah 39:1-10

Let's find out!

✦   Are the people going home?
✦   Why is this happening?

Lord Jesus, I am sorry that these people did wrong, and You had to punish them. Help me to do only those things that please You and make You happy.

Jonah Runs Away

THIS MAN'S NAME IS JONAH. He is running away from God. God has told him to go to a big city and tell the people there to stop being bad. Jonah is afraid to go. He is afraid the people will hurt him if he tells them what God said. So now he is running away instead of doing what God told him to. He is getting on a ship to sail far, far away to another country. He thinks God will not find him there. But nobody can run away from God. Jonah should know that. You know it, don't you?

Jonah 1:1-3

Let's find out!

- ✦ Where is Jonah going?
- ✦ Is he obeying God?
- ✦ What did God want Jonah to do?

Lord Jesus, I don't want to hide from You like Jonah tried to do. I want to stay with You, and I want You to stay with me.

Swallowed by a Big Fish

WHO IS THIS MAN SWIMMING IN THE WATER? It is Jonah. He was in that boat and a big storm came along. All the men in the boat prayed to God to help them. They asked God to keep their boat from sinking. Then Jonah told them to throw him into the water and the storm would go away. He said he was running away from God and that God had sent the storm to punish him. The men were sad, but they did what Jonah said and threw him out of the boat into the water and now the storm is going away. Jonah is in the water but God won't let him die. He has sent a great fish to swallow Jonah without hurting him. Do you see the fish? After three days this fish will swim over to the beach with Jonah inside and spit Jonah out onto the sand. After that Jonah will do whatever God tells him to.

Jonah 1:3-17

Let's find out!

✦ Why is Jonah in the water?
✦ How long will Jonah be inside the fish?

Thank You, Lord, for helping Jonah decide to do what You told him.

Jonah Preaches in Nineveh

HERE IS ANOTHER PICTURE OF JONAH, the man who ran away from God and was swallowed by a big fish. After the fish had spit him out onto the dry ground, God spoke again to Jonah and told him to go to the city of Nineveh and to preach to the people there. "Jonah," God said, "tell the people who live in Nineveh that they have been bad and I will need to punish them next month." Here in this picture you can see Jonah doing what God told him to. He is telling all the people what God said. The people are listening. They are sorry and afraid. Now they will stop doing bad things because they know God will punish them if they keep on doing them. Now God will not need to punish these people because they are listening to Jonah. Aren't you glad that Jonah did not try to run away again?

Jonah 3:1-10

Let's find out!

✦ What is Jonah telling the people?

✦ Will God need to punish these people now?

I'm glad Jonah and the people all listened to You, Father God; I know that made You happy.

Daniel and the King's Food

NOW I AM GOING TO TELL YOU a very wonderful story about a boy named Daniel. The king has sent some very good food for Daniel to eat, but Daniel won't eat it. In the picture you can see him telling the two men to take the food away. Shall I tell you why? Daniel doesn't want to eat the good food because the king doesn't believe in God. The king prays to idols. An idol is a statue that looks like a man, but it is not alive. When the king asks the blessing at the table, he doesn't ask God to bless the food. Instead the king prays to idols and asks them to bless it. Daniel doesn't want to eat food blessed by idols, even if it is cake and candy and ice cream. Daniel wants God to be happy, more than he wants to eat the best food. Daniel would rather have oatmeal or soup blessed by God than to have cake the king has asked idols to bless.

Daniel 1:3-17

Let's find out!

+ Who is this boy?
+ What is happening in this picture?

Daniel pleased You, Lord. I want to do right and make You happy, too.

The Hand Writes on the Wall

*T*HE KING HAS MANY FRIENDS with him eating lots of good food. But do you see something very strange in this picture? Can you see where Daniel is pointing? Do you see the hand on the wall writing strange letters? No one is there, only a hand. Where does the hand come from? It must be an angel's hand, or perhaps the hand of God that is writing these letters. The king does not know what they mean. Daniel is pointing to the letters and reading them to the king. Daniel tells the king that God is angry and that the king can't be the king anymore. God won't let him.

Daniel 5:1-17

Let's find out!

- ✦ Whose hand is writing the letters on the wall?

- ✦ Who is telling the king what the letters mean?

Father God, thank You for telling the king what the letters on the wall meant, and thank You for the Bible because it tells us what to do.

The Men Watch Daniel Praying

*D*ANIEL IS PRAYING. That is good because God is hearing his prayer and will do what Daniel asks. But do you see the men hiding outside Daniel's door? What are they doing there? They are listening to Daniel. They want to know whether he is praying to God. They say that Daniel must not pray to God. They will hurt him if he does. Daniel knows the men are there listening but he doesn't care. He prays to God anyway. He would rather pray to God even if the men hurt him.

Daniel 6:1-11

Let's find out!

✦ What is Daniel doing?
✦ What are the men doing?

Thank You, Lord Jesus, for making Daniel brave and strong to do what was right.

Daniel Is Put
with the Lions

*T*HE MEN HAVE PUT DANIEL IN WITH ALL OF THESE LIONS. Why did they do this? It is because Daniel was praying to God. The king had said not to pray to God. The men told the king, "Daniel is praying!" So the king punished Daniel by throwing him into this cave where the hungry lions were kept. Will the lions eat Daniel? No, God has sent His angel to take care of him. The angel will keep the lions' mouths shut so that they cannot hurt Daniel. He prays to God and God is taking care of him.

Daniel 6:10-23

Let's find out!

✦ Why is Daniel there with the lions?

✦ Will the lions hurt him?

Dear Lord, thank You for keeping Daniel safe from the lions. Please keep me safe and help me to love You like Daniel did.

THE NEW TESTAMENT
In Pictures
FOR
Little Eyes

Angels Tell of Jesus' Birth

IT IS NIGHTTIME AND THESE MEN ARE OUT in the fields taking care of their sheep. They chase the bears away so that they will not eat the sheep. Can you see their sheep? But now what is happening? Who are these angels who have come? What are they saying? They are telling these men that God's Son has been born that night. He is a little baby. The angels are glad and the men are glad. They go quickly to the place where the baby is, so that they can pray to Him and thank God for Him.

Luke 2:1-15

Let's find out!

+ Why are the men outside at night?
+ What are the angels telling them?
+ What do they decide to do?

Dear Father God, the angels were glad, and the shepherds were glad, and I am glad that Your Son was born into the world. Thank You for Your Son, Jesus.

Shepherds Visit Baby Jesus

*T*HE MEN WHO WERE TAKING CARE OF THE SHEEP have come to find God's Son. The angels told them where to find Him and now they have come to see the baby Jesus. There is the baby and His mother. The mother's name is Mary. God is the baby's Father. The men who are taking care of the sheep are worshiping the baby and thanking God that the baby is God's Son. The baby's name is Jesus.

Luke 2:16-18

Let's find out!

- ✦ Who is this baby?
- ✦ Who is the baby's Father?
- ✦ What is His mother's name?

Thank You, Lord God, for telling the men—and for telling me too —that Jesus is Your Son.

Wise Men Follow the Star

WHO ARE THESE MEN? They are riding on camels. Have you ever seen a camel? Where are the men going in such a hurry? They are going to find God's Son. God has told them that His Son is going to be born. They are bringing many gifts to give Him. They know where to go because God has sent a star for them to follow. The star will take them to the baby Jesus.

Matthew 2:1-9

Let's find out!

✦ Where are the men going?

✦ How do they know where to go?

✦ What is the name of God's Son?

Dear Father God, thank You that these men listened when You told them to go to worship Jesus. Help me to worship Him, too.

Wise Men Give Their Gifts

*T*HE MEN WHO WERE ON THE CAMELS have come a long way from another country. Now they have found the little baby they were looking for. They know that the baby is God's Son. They have brought many gifts to give Him. They are holding them out for Him to see while they worship Him and thank God. God is kind to these men to let them see His Son Jesus.

Matthew 2:10,11

Let's find out!

✦ Are the men giving presents to the baby Jesus?

✦ How many presents can you count?

Thank You, Lord, for wanting people from faraway places to know Jesus, too.

Simeon Holds Baby Jesus

CAN YOU SEE THE OLD MAN in the picture who is holding the baby? He has waited all his life to see God's baby Son. The old man has asked Mary if he can hold Jesus. He has never been so happy in all his life before, because now at last Jesus is born and he can hold Him in his arms. He knows that Jesus will take care of God's people. The name of the woman standing behind him is Anna. God has told her, too, that this baby is His Son and she is very, very happy.

Luke 2:25-38

Let's find out!

✦ Why are the man and the lady so happy?

✦ Is Jesus God's Son?

Father God, thank You for making these people so happy by sending Jesus to help people everywhere. I am happy about this, too. Thank You!

Jesus Visits the Temple

*T*HIS IS ANOTHER PICTURE OF JESUS. He has become a big boy now. In this picture we see the big men He is talking to. These old men are preachers and teachers. The boy Jesus is asking them questions and telling them things about God. These men cannot understand how a boy can know so much about God. They do not know that this boy is God's Son. This is Jesus.

Luke 2:40-52

Let's find out!

✦ Who is this boy?

✦ Why are the men surprised?

✦ Why does the boy know so much about God?

Dear Lord, I'm glad I know why the boy Jesus knew so much—He's Your Son!

John Baptizes Jesus

*T*HIS IS ANOTHER PICTURE OF JESUS. Now He is a man. Another man whose name is John is pointing up to God and praying. John will baptize Jesus. Jesus is glad because God wants John to do this. As soon as Jesus is baptized He will hear a voice from the sky saying, "This is my Son and I love Him. Listen to what He tells you to do." Do you know where the voice will come from? It will be God talking to Jesus and the other people who are watching him. God wants everyone to know that this is His Son.

Matthew 3:13-17

Let's find out!

+ What is John doing to Jesus?
+ Where will the voice come from?
+ What will the voice say?

Father God, thank You for letting me know that Jesus is Your Son.

Jesus Says No to Satan

JESUS HAS GONE FAR AWAY. There are no other people here to help Him or to make Him happy. He is alone. He has not eaten anything for breakfast, or lunch, or supper. He did not eat anything yesterday or the day before that. He has not eaten anything for forty days. Soon Satan, God's enemy, will come and try to get Jesus to do something bad but Jesus will not listen to bad Satan. Jesus is God's Son and He is good. He has never done anything bad at all. He will never listen to Satan. Jesus listens only to God His Father and does only what God says.

Matthew 4:1-11

Let's find out!

✦ Why is Jesus hungry?

✦ Will He ever do anything bad?

✦ Who will try to get Jesus to be bad?

Lord Jesus, thank You for always doing what is right. Help me to be like Jesus and always do right.

Jesus Chooses His Helpers

JESUS ASKS TWELVE MEN to be His special friends. These men are called His disciples. They go with Jesus wherever He goes and help Him in all His work. These men are happy because Jesus has asked them to help Him. Some of the names of these men are Peter, John, James, Thomas, and Andrew. These twelve men are Jesus' helpers.

Mark 3:13-19

Let's find out!

✦ Who are these men?

✦ Will they help Jesus?

✦ Do you know any of their names?

Dear Lord Jesus, thank You that You want me to be Your friend, and to help You in Your work.

Jesus Changes Water to Wine

*O*NE DAY JESUS WAS AT A BIG DINNER at a wedding. After a while the people eating dinner needed more wine to drink. Jesus told the servants to fill up six big jars with water, and take them to the man who was in charge of the dinner. And do you know what? It wasn't water any more. It was better wine than they had ever tasted. Jesus can do things like that because He is God.

John 2:1-11

Let's find out!

+ What did the people ask Jesus to do?
+ What did Jesus tell them to do with the big jars?
+ Can Jesus help us when we need Him?

Thank You, Lord Jesus, that You can give me anything I need, because You are God.

Men Buy and Sell in God's House

JESUS IS MAKING SOME MEN get out of God's house. They didn't come to God's house to love God and pray. No, they are doing things there that God does not want them to do. They are selling things to get a lot of money and be rich. They don't love God. Jesus has a whip in His hand and the men are afraid of Him. He tells them to take all of those things away. He says that they are in His Father's house and they must not do things like that when they are there.

John 2:13-17

Let's find out!

✦ What does Jesus have in His hand?
✦ What does Jesus want these men to do?

Help me, Lord, to think about You when I am at church, and not about playing or other things.

Peter Catches Many Fish

*D*O YOU SEE JESUS STANDING THERE? He told Peter to throw his fishing net in the water. Peter did not think that there would be any fish but he did what Jesus told him, and now just see how many fish there are! Peter obeyed Jesus and now Peter has all these fish. Can you see all the fish? There are almost too many to count. Peter and his friends don't know what to do with all of them. They have so many in their boat that it is almost sinking. They give some to the men in another boat and it is almost sinking too. Why did all these fish come into the net?

Luke 5:1-11

Let's find out!

+ Who told Peter to catch the fish?
+ Can you count how many fish there are, or are there too many?

Lord Jesus, thank You for showing Peter that You are Somebody special. Thank You that I know this, too.

Men Bring a Sick Friend to Jesus

WHAT IS HAPPENING HERE? Look at the men at the top of the picture. They brought their friend to Jesus. They have taken away part of the roof of the house and lowered him down through the roof, right in front of Jesus, where Jesus will be sure to see him. The man could not walk and was lying on his bed. Can you see his bed? They brought him to Jesus because they want him to walk again. Jesus tells the man to get well and now he is standing up. Jesus made him well right away.

Luke 5:17-26

Let's find out!

◆ How did the men get their friend down to Jesus?

◆ What did Jesus do to make the man walk again?

Thank You, Lord Jesus, for healing this man, so that he could walk again. How wonderful and powerful You are.

Nicodemus Talks to Jesus

IT IS NIGHTTIME and Jesus is talking to a man whose name is Nicodemus. Can you say, "Nicodemus"? He is a good man but he does not know that Jesus is God's Son and he doesn't know very much about God. Jesus is telling him about God. He is telling him how to get to heaven. He says, "Nicodemus, you cannot get there by yourself but God will take you there if you believe in Me. God loves you, Nicodemus." Jesus died so that Nicodemus could go to heaven. Jesus died so that you and I can go to heaven if we love Him.

John 3:1-5, 14-18

Let's find out!

✦ What is this man's name?
✦ Did he know God?
✦ Why did Jesus have to die?

Dear Lord, I'm so sorry that You had to die, but thank You for making a way for me to live in heaven with You someday.

A Little Boy Is Well Again

*T*HIS MAN IS GLAD because his little boy feels all better again. Yesterday he was so sick that he didn't want to run and play. He only wanted to be there in his bed. His father was sad. He went to see Jesus. He asked Jesus to come and make the little boy well. Jesus said that He would help. He told the father to go home and the little boy would be all right. Jesus is far away but He makes the little boy well again.

John 4:46-54

Let's find out!

✦ Was the little boy sick?

✦ Is he sick now?

✦ Jesus is not here in the picture. Where is He?

Lord Jesus, thank You for making this boy well again, even though You were far away.

Jesus Teaches the People

JESUS IS TALKING TO THE PEOPLE. See how many of them there are! They want to hear what Jesus says. They know Jesus is their Friend and they want to do what He tells them. He is telling the people to be kind and good. He tells them not to quarrel. Some of these people will love Jesus always and some of them will go away from Him and not want Him to be their Friend anymore. If Jesus is not their Friend, then God will not let them come to heaven. Jesus wants to be your Friend too. If you want Him to be your friend, tell Him so now.

Matthew 5:1-11

Let's find out!

✦ Who is talking to the people?
✦ Is Jesus your Friend?

Even today, some people don't want to be Your friend, Lord, but I do. Help me to do the kind things You want me to do.

Two Men Build Houses

JESUS TOLD A STORY ABOUT TWO MEN who built houses. One of them built his house on the sand. He was a foolish man. It rained and rained and all of the sand washed away and the house fell down. The other man built his house on a rock. Even though it rains and rains, the rock and the house will not wash away. He is a wise man because he built his house on a rock.

Matthew 7:24-29

Let's find out!

✦ Was it a good idea to build a house on the sand?

✦ What happened to that house?

✦ When it rained did the house on the rock fall down?

Lord Jesus, help me to be smart and wise by always trusting You and doing what You tell me to do.

Jesus Makes
a Dead Man Live

JESUS IS HELPING A MAN SIT UP. The man was dead and his mother was sad. Jesus saw the mother crying. He went over to see the man lying on the bed. The man could not move. He was dead. Jesus tells him to be alive again. When Jesus says that, all of a sudden the man begins to move. He opens his eyes and sees Jesus and he sees his mother too. The man and his mother are glad and Jesus is glad too.

Luke 7:11-16

Let's find out!

✦ Was the man dead?
✦ What did Jesus tell him to do?
✦ Then what happened?

Dear Lord Jesus, You are God, and that is why You could make the dead man come back to life again. Thank You for doing this.

Jesus Stops a Storm

JESUS AND HIS FRIENDS ARE IN A BOAT. It is at night. There is a great storm. The wind is blowing. It is raining hard. The friends are afraid the ship will sink and they will all be drowned. Is Jesus afraid? No, He isn't. No, because He knows His God will take care of them. Jesus is standing up and holding up His hands and now the storm is going away. Jesus tells the storm to stop and it does.

Matthew 8:23-27

Let's find out!

✦ Is Jesus afraid?
✦ What is He doing?
✦ What will happen to the storm?

I thank You, Lord, that even the wind and the water do what You say.

Jesus Makes a Dead Girl Live

*T*HIS LITTLE GIRL IS TWELVE YEARS OLD. She was very sick and her father went to find Jesus. He asked Jesus to come and make his little girl well again. The doctors couldn't get her better, but he knows Jesus can. Jesus comes and takes the little girl's hand and says, "Get up, little girl." Right away she sits up and gets out of bed and starts to play and she is all right again. The little girl died but Jesus brought her back to life and gave her to her mother and father. That is why they are so surprised and happy.

Mark 5:22-43

Let's find out!

✦ Why are the mother and father so happy?

✦ How did Jesus make the little girl well?

Dear Lord, thank You for making the girl alive again after she died.

A Blind Man Sees Again

JESUS IS TALKING HERE WITH A MAN who cannot see Him. The man is blind. His eyes are hurt so that he cannot see anything at all. Close your eyes now and you can tell what it is like to be blind. Everything is dark. Someone told this man Jesus was coming. The man heard Jesus coming. Then he cried out very loudly, "Jesus, please help me. Please make my eyes well so that I can see." Jesus touches his eyes and says, "Be open." And right away his eyes are all right and he can see. Isn't Jesus a wonderful Friend?

Matthew 9:27-31

Let's find out!

✦ Could the man see Jesus?
✦ What did Jesus say to make his eyes open?

Thank You, Lord, for telling the blind man's eyes to see again.

A Man Is a Good Neighbor

*T*HIS POOR MAN LYING ON THE GROUND was going on a trip, and all of a sudden some men came and took away his money and some of his clothes and hurt him and ran away. They left him lying there on the road. Then the pastor of a church came walking along but didn't stop to help him. He just looked at him and went on. Then another man from a church came along. He didn't help him either. Then a man he didn't like came along and stopped. You can see him in the picture helping the poor man who is hurt. He is pouring some medicine on some hurt places, and soon he will lift him up and put him on his donkey and take him to a hotel. Jesus wants us to be kind to everyone, even people who hit us or don't like us.

Luke 10:30-37

Let's find out!

- ✦ Why is the man lying there?
- ✦ What is the other man doing?

Dear Father God, help me to be a good helper.

Mary Listens to Jesus Teach

MARY IS SITTING LISTENING while Jesus talks to her. He is telling her many things that she needs to know. Do you see the other lady, the one who is standing up? Her name is Martha. She is Mary's sister. She is getting supper ready. Martha is working very hard and wants Mary to help her instead of talking to Jesus. Martha asks Jesus to make Mary help her get the supper. But Jesus says, "No, let Mary sit here and listen, because that is even more important than getting supper." Jesus meant that we should not always be working and playing, but should take time to talk to Him and listen to Him.

Luke 10:38-42

Let's find out!

- ✦ Who are these two ladies?
- ✦ What does the one standing up want the other one to do?
- ✦ Did Jesus say that Mary should keep on listening to Him?

Help me, Lord Jesus, to listen carefully to the stories from the Bible, and then do what You say.

Jesus Talks with Bad Leaders

JESUS IS ANGRY WITH THESE MEN. He is talking to them while they are eating their dinners. He is angry because they say that they love God and they really don't. They say that they want to obey God, but they are telling lies because they want to do things their own way instead of the way God says. They give money to God but they do not love Him. They go to God's house but they do not love God. That is why Jesus is angry. He wants them to love God. He does not want their money unless they love Him.

Luke 11:37-44

Let's find out!

- ✦ Why is Jesus angry with these men?
- ✦ Do these men love God?
- ✦ Do they give money to God?
- ✦ Does God want their money if they do not love Him?

Dear Father God, please help me to love and obey You, as well as giving my money to You.

A Rich Farmer Forgets God

*T*HIS MAN IS A RICH FARMER. He has lots of money. He is looking at his barns. Do you see his men putting hay into the barns? But this man does not love God. He loves his money and his farm more than he loves God. He has so much money and food that he doesn't know where to put it so he is going to build a bigger barn. But tonight God will let this rich man die so he will not wake up tomorrow morning. He can't use all his food in the barn anymore because he will die tonight and never come back. God will take him away. The man is bad because he loves his farm but doesn't love God.

Luke 12:16-21

Let's find out!

+ Does this man have lots of things?
+ Does this man love God?

Lord God, I love my toys, and help me to love You more than toys or anything else.

Jesus Teaches about God's Care

JESUS IS TALKING TO HIS FRIENDS. Do you see the pretty flower He is pointing to? Jesus is telling them to look at the flowers. The flowers don't work hard to cook their suppers, do they? No, flowers don't need to cook and work hard, because God takes care of them. They don't need fine clothes, because God has made them grow with their beautiful clothes right on them. Jesus is telling His friends that God takes care of the flowers and He will take care of them too if they ask Him, and if they do whatever He says.

Luke 12:27-32

Let's find out!

+ What is Jesus showing the disciples?
+ Will God take care of you?

Father God, please help me to remember that I can make You happy by obeying You.

A Man Sows Seed

*T*HIS MAN IS PLANTING SEEDS. He is carrying them in his bag over his shoulder. He throws the little seeds out on the ground. He wants them to grow into little plants that will grow up into tall stalks of wheat. But look! Do you see the birds behind him? They are eating up some of the seeds. Those seeds will not grow because the birds are taking them away. Some of the seed is falling down on the rocks and thorns. Can you see the thorns? The seeds cannot grow there very well. But some of the seeds fall on good ground and will grow up and become big plants.

Matthew 13:3-8

Let's find out!

✦ Will the seed grow on the rock?
✦ Where will the seed grow best?

Dear Lord, please help me keep on growing strong like the little plants.

A Boy Shares
His Bread and Fish

*L*OOK AT ALL THESE PEOPLE. See how many there are? They are all hungry. They had not had any lunch and now it is time for supper and they don't have anything to eat. One boy brought his lunch so he will not be hungry. He would be glad to give his lunch to all the people but do you think that would be enough for them to eat? No, of course not. The boy is giving his lunch to Jesus. Jesus will break the bread in pieces and give the pieces to His helpers, and do you know what will happen then? Jesus made the five pieces of bread in his lunch become enough bread for all the people to eat as much as they wanted, with a lot left over!

Matthew 14:15-23

Let's find out!

✦ What is the boy doing with his lunch?
✦ What will Jesus do with it?

Thank You, Lord Jesus, that You can use even boys and girls to help other people. Please use me to be Your helper.

Jesus Walks on the Water

WHAT IS HAPPENING IN THIS PICTURE? There is water with a boat in it and there are some men in the boat. Do you see Jesus in the picture? Is He swimming in the water? No, He is walking on top of it. Can you walk on top of water in your bathtub? No, of course not. But Jesus made the water. He can stand on it if He wants to. One of the men in the boat is Peter. When Peter sees Jesus on the water he wants to walk on it too. Peter will step out on the water and start to walk toward Jesus. Then Peter will become frightened and begin to sink, and Jesus will come and save him.

Matthew 14:22-33

Let's find out!

- ✦ Can Jesus walk on top of the water?
- ✦ Will Peter walk part of the way on top of the water?
- ✦ When Peter gets scared, then what will happen?

Lord, help me to trust You, so that You can help me do whatever You tell me to.

Jesus' Clothes Are Shiny

*J*ESUS IS TALKING TO PETER AND JAMES AND JOHN. They are up on a high mountain. No one else is there. All of a sudden Jesus' clothes begin to shine and become brighter and brighter, and whiter than snow. Peter and James and John are frightened. Then all of a sudden they see two other men standing there talking to Jesus. You can see them there in the picture. These two men are Moses and Elijah who lived long ago. They have come down from heaven to talk to Jesus. They are talking about how some bad men are going to take Jesus and hurt Him and kill Him. Soon Moses and Elijah will go away again and a bright cloud will come over above where Jesus is standing. God's voice will talk out of the cloud and say, "Jesus is My Son, listen to Him."

Matthew 17:1-9

Let's find out!

+ What color did Jesus' clothes become?
+ Who came to talk with Jesus?
+ What did the voice in the cloud say?

Father God, thank You that I know Jesus is Your Son, and I want to do whatever He tells me to.

298

Jesus Makes Lazarus Live

LAZARUS IS JESUS' FRIEND. One day Lazarus got sick and died. Jesus wasn't there to make him well again. The friends of Lazarus took his body and put it in the hole in the big rock and covered the hole so that no one could go in or out. When Jesus came He told the men to roll away the stone, and Jesus prayed and asked God to make Lazarus alive. Now can you see what is happening in this picture? Lazarus is coming out again. He was dead but now he is alive. Do you know why? It is because Jesus is there.

John 11:1-45

Let's find out!

✦ Did Jesus make the man alive?
✦ Are the people glad that Jesus came?

Thank You, Lord, for making Your friend Lazarus alive again. Thank You that someday You will make all Your friends who die become alive again.

Jesus Loves Children

JESUS LOVES LITTLE CHILDREN. In this picture He is holding some of them on His lap and talking to them. Once Jesus' friends tried to send the children away. They thought that Jesus didn't want children around Him. Jesus talked to the disciples and told them never to say things like that. He wants the children to be with Him. He says, "Let the little children come to Me. Do not send them away because I love them and want them with Me."

Matthew 19:13-15

Let's find out!

✦ What is Jesus holding in His arms?
✦ Does Jesus love little children?
✦ Are you a little child?
✦ Does Jesus love you?

Dear Lord Jesus, thank You so much for telling us that You love boys and girls like me. I love You, too.

Jesus Cries about a City

JESUS IS CRYING. He is looking at the old city of Jerusalem. There are many people in this city where He is looking. They do not love Jesus or His Father. They do not know that Jesus is God's Son. Jesus knows that some day a great army will come and knock down their city. If these people would only believe in Jesus then these terrible things would not happen to them. Jesus loves them and wants to help them, but they do not love Jesus and that is why He is crying.

Luke 13:31-35

Let's find out!

✦ What is Jesus looking at?

✦ Why is He crying?

Lord, I don't want You to be sad, so please help more people find out that You are God's Son. Then they can believe in You and You can love and help them.

A Shepherd Finds His Lost Sheep

*T*HE MAN IN THE PICTURE has lost one of his sheep. It ran away and fell down and couldn't get back up again. The little sheep is lost and crying and helpless. The man went to find it and finally he is there picking it up. He will take it home and get it all warm again and get it something to eat. The man in the picture is good because he takes care of the sheep. Jesus is like that man. Jesus wants to take care of us when we get lost. Jesus loves you very much. You can be one of His little lambs.

Luke 15:3-7

Let's find out!

✦ How did the little sheep get there?

✦ What is the man doing?

Thank You, Jesus, that You love me even more than this man loved his sheep.

Perfume for Jesus

*T*HIS YOUNG WOMAN IS PUTTING PERFUME ON JESUS' feet and then wiping it off with her hair. The perfume has cost a lot of money. The men sitting at the table with Jesus are telling Him that the lady shouldn't do this, but Jesus is glad. He wants her to do this because she is doing it to tell Jesus, "Thank You." Jesus has been kind to her. She has done many bad things but Jesus will forgive her. Jesus will die for her sins. She is glad that He is so kind and so she had put the perfume on His feet to tell Him, "Thank You." Jesus died for you, too. Have you told Him, "Thank You"?

John 12:1-7

Let's find out!

✦ Where did the woman put the perfume?

✦ Was Jesus glad?

✦ Have you ever told Jesus, "Thank You," for what He has done for you?

✦ Shall we thank Him now?

I thank You, Lord Jesus, that You died to take away God's punishment for the bad things I have done.

A Boy Goes Away from Home

*T*HIS BOY IS GOING AWAY FROM HOME. He is saying good-by to his father. His father is sorry because he doesn't want the son to go away. But his son thinks it will be more fun away from home. He asked his father to give him a lot of money and now he will go away. Are you sorry that the boy is doing this? He should have stayed at home and worked and helped his father instead of going away.

Luke 15:11-19

Let's find out!

✦ Did the man's son want to stay home or go away?

✦ Is the father happy or sad?

When I do things that make You sad, Father God, help me be quick to say, "I'm sorry."

A Boy Goes Back to His Father

*I*N THIS PICTURE YOU CAN SEE the man who went away from his house even when his father didn't want him to. Now he has come back home again. His father is very happy. After he went away he began to get very hungry and so he decided to come home again. His father is glad to see him. He didn't know if his father would want him to come back, but you can see how happy the father is to see him again. When the father saw him he ran and welcomed him and is telling him how glad he is.

Luke 15:20-24

Let's find out!

✦ Did the father let the boy come home?

✦ Is the boy happy?

✦ Is the father happy?

Thank You, Lord, that You aren't angry when I tell You I'm sorry. You're happy to see me come to You.

One Man Thanks Jesus

*D*O YOU SEE THESE MEN who are walking away from Jesus? They were men with leprosy. That means that they were very sick. Everyone was afraid to go near them because they were so sick. People who touched them might get sick too. When they saw Jesus they called to Him and said, "Jesus, help us. Please help us." Jesus saw them and heard them calling. He wanted to help them and He made all of them well. He healed them all but only one of them came back to tell Him, "Thank You." This man is so glad he is well again that he falls down in front of Jesus. All the others forgot to tell Jesus, "Thank You."

Luke 17:11-19

Let's find out!

- ✦ Were all these men sick?
- ✦ Who healed them?
- ✦ What is the man in the picture doing?
- ✦ Have you thanked Jesus because He is your Friend?

I want to thank You right now, Lord Jesus, that You are my Friend.

Jesus Tells about Some Grape Growers

WHY IS THIS MAN LYING HERE SO STILL? It is because he is dead. His father owns that house but some other people are living there. His father sent his son to get the rent money from the people staying in the house but the people wouldn't give the money to him. Instead they hurt him and killed him and threw him out on the ground where you can see him lying. What do you think the father will do when he hears about this? He will see to it that these men are killed because of the terrible thing they have done to his son.

Matthew 21:33-41

Let's find out!

+ Who owns this house?
+ What did the man's father send him to get?
+ What did the people do?

Father God, everything You give me is Yours. Help me to remember this and always be ready to give it back to You.

A Poor Woman Gives to God

JESUS IS SITTING IN GOD'S HOUSE watching the people putting money into a box. They are giving this money to God. In the picture you can see a woman who doesn't have very much money. She has brought a few pennies. That is all the money she has, and she is giving it all to God. When she puts this in she will not have any more money left at all. She is giving God everything that she has. Jesus is glad because she loves God so much. He doesn't think the rich men standing there have given very much at all. They have put in lots more money but they are still rich and have lots more money left for themselves at home. Jesus says the poor woman's few pennies are better than all the money from the rich people who don't love Him.

Mark 12:41-44

Let's find out!

✦ Did the rich men put in a lot of money?
✦ How much does the poor woman have left after she puts in her money?

I can't do a lot for You, Lord, but I can please You by obeying. I want to do that.

318

Jesus Rides into the City

*E*VERYONE IS HAPPY because Jesus has come to visit them. He has come to the city of Jerusalem. All the people think he has come to Jerusalem to be their king. They want Jesus to be king because He is so kind to them and can help them. See how some people are putting their coats on the ground for Jesus to ride over. Others are cutting down branches from the trees and making a path for Him. The people shout and thank God because they think Jesus will help them all be rich and have lots of money and other things that they don't have now. They do not know that Jesus will soon be killed.

John 12:12-19

Let's find out!

+ Are the people happy?
+ What are they putting down on the road for Jesus to ride over?
+ Why are they doing this?

Thank You that I know why You came, Lord Jesus: You came to die for our sins.

Jesus Tells What Will Happen to Him

*H*ERE IN THIS PICTURE YOU CAN SEE JESUS talking to some of His friends. He is telling them about what is going to happen to Him. He is pointing up to Heaven, telling them that soon He will go there to be with God His Father. Jesus says that some day all His friends will come to heaven too and live there with Him always.

Luke 22:14-22

Let's find out!

✦ Where is Jesus pointing?
✦ What is He telling His friends?

Lord, thank You for inviting me to come and live with You in heaven someday.

A Great Dinner

*T*HIS MAN HAS MADE A GREAT DINNER and is ready to eat it. Can you see the man pointing to the food on the table? But who is coming to eat it? The man asked many of his rich friends to come and have dinner with him but they wouldn't. They didn't know what a wonderful dinner it was going to be so they said they had other things to do and couldn't come. Then the man invited the poor people who were sick and crippled and blind. Do you see them coming? They are glad to come and eat. Soon the table will be full of people. The man is glad because of his new friends but he is sorry because of those who would not come. Jesus wants you to come and live with Him some day. Will you be glad to come?

Matthew 22:1-14

Let's find out!

+ Who did the man invite at first to come and eat the good dinner?

+ Who finally came to the dinner?

+ Does Jesus want you to come to Him?

Lord Jesus, thank You for inviting me. I'll be glad to come!

Jesus Talks about Loving God

SOME MEN ARE ASKING JESUS A QUESTION. They want to know what is the most important rule for them to obey. Can you think what that rule would be? Would it be to eat nicely? Or would it be not going across the street alone? No. These things are very important and you should eat nicely and must be careful about cars or you will get into trouble. But there is something even more important that we should do. Jesus tells these men what it is. He says that the greatest thing for them to do is to always love God. Do you love God? Do you do whatever He says? What are some things God wants you to do?

Matthew 22:35-40

Let's find out!

✦ What is the most important rule to obey?

✦ What are some things God wants you to do?

✦ Do you love God by doing what He says?

Dear Father God, help me to love You in the very best way—by doing what You tell me in Your book.

326

Jesus Eats His Last Supper

*W*HAT IS HAPPENING IN THIS PICTURE? Jesus has a loaf of bread in His hand. He is breaking it into pieces. He will give these pieces to His disciples who are sitting there at the supper table. Jesus will tell them to eat the bread. He says that the bread is His body. Jesus is telling His disciples that He must soon die. He died for you. He died for me. We have done bad things that God must punish. But Jesus asked to be punished for you. God punished Jesus instead of you. Jesus didn't do anything bad but God punished Him. Do you know why?

Luke 22:14-20

Let's find out!

✦   What does Jesus have in His hand?
✦   Who will eat the bread?
✦   What is going to happen to Jesus?

Thank You, thank You, Jesus,
for being punished instead of me.

328

Jesus Teaches about Heaven

JESUS IS TALKING TO HIS DISCIPLES. He is telling them what is going to happen to Him. Some men are going to take Him and kill Him but Jesus tells them not to be afraid. He says that God will take care of them. Jesus tells them that He will go away to His Father, away up in heaven. When He gets there He will get places ready for them to come to live. He is getting a place ready for you to live in heaven too, if you love Jesus.

John 14:1-14

Let's find out!

✦ What is Jesus telling them?
✦ Where is Jesus now?

Lord Jesus, I'm so glad to hear that You are getting a place ready in heaven for all Your people.

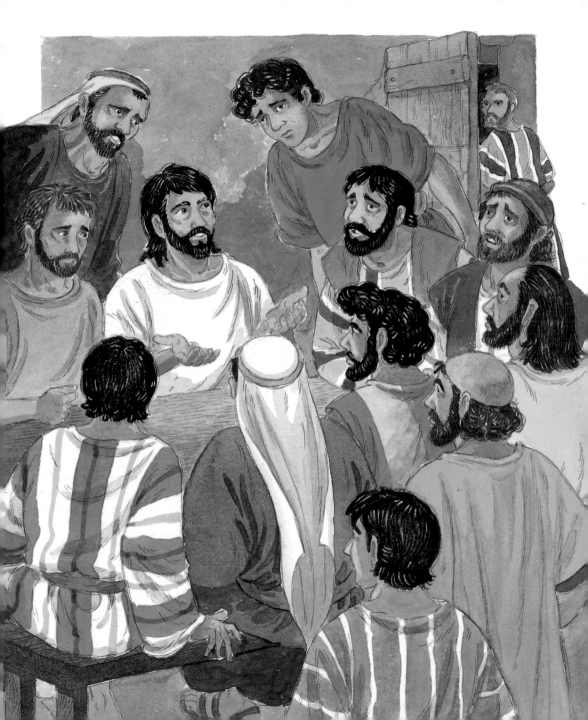

Jesus Prays in the Garden

JESUS IS PRAYING ALL ALONE. He is in a garden and it is night. He is talking to His Father in heaven. Jesus is very, very sad because He knows what will happen to Him soon. He knows that some men will come to get Him and take Him away and nail Him to a cross so that He will die. He will die on the cross so that God will not need to punish you and me for the bad things we have done. Jesus is sad because He does not want to die. He doesn't need to, either. He could ask God to send the angels to take care of Him but He will let the men kill Him. Jesus is glad to die for you.

Luke 22:39-48

Let's find out!

✦ Is Jesus happy or sad?

✦ What is going to happen to Him?

I'm sorry You had to die, Lord,
but I know You did it for me.
Thank You so very much.

Judas Shows Where Jesus Is

*D*ID YOU EVER HEAR about a man named Judas Iscariot? Judas pretended that he was one of Jesus' friends. Some bad men said they would give Judas money if he would help them catch Jesus. In this picture Judas is bringing them to where Jesus is. It is night. They are bringing torches. Do you see the torches in their hands, giving light? They don't have flashlights and so they use these torches instead. Is Jesus going to run away from them? No, Jesus is standing, waiting. He could go away if He wanted to, but He will let them take Him.

Luke 22:47-54

Let's find out!

✦ What is the name of the man leading these bad people to Jesus?

✦ Why doesn't Jesus run away?

I don't want to be like Judas, Lord Jesus. Help me never to say You are not my friend.

Peter Tells a Lie

PETER IS ONE OF JESUS' friends and disciples. He is getting warm by being near the fire with some of Jesus' enemies. The woman is pointing at him but he is telling her, "No." Why is he saying that? She has asked Peter if Jesus is his Friend. He says that he doesn't know Jesus at all. What a bad thing to say. Peter is telling a lie because he is afraid the other people there will hurt him if they know he is Jesus' friend. Soon he will look up and see Jesus looking at him and then he will cry because he has done such a bad thing.

Luke 22:60-62

Let's find out!

✦ Was Peter a friend of Jesus?
✦ What did Peter tell the girl?

Lord, when I feel like telling a lie, make me strong to say only what is true.

Pilate Listens to the People

NOW THE PEOPLE HAVE TAKEN JESUS to a man whose name is Pilate. Pilate can let them kill Jesus or else make them let Jesus go. He is talking to the people and telling them that he thinks he ought to let Jesus go. He says Jesus is good. He tells them that Jesus hasn't done anything bad at all. See how angry the people are! They want Pilate to let them kill Jesus. They are shouting at Pilate and Pilate is afraid of them. Soon he will decide to give Jesus to the men so they can kill Him.

John 19:1-16

Let's find out!

✦   What is this man's name?
✦   What do the people want Pilate to do?
✦   What will Pilate do?

Father God, sometimes I feel like doing wrong things. When that happens, please help me to do what is right.

Jesus Is Put on the Cross

*T*HE BAD MEN HAVE TAKEN Jesus up the hill and have nailed His hands and His feet on these big pieces of wood so that He will die after a while. Can you think what it would be like if you were hanging there with nails through your hands? Oh, what a terrible thing they are doing to Jesus! Do you know why Jesus was nailed there? It is because He loves you and me. You and I have done bad things and God should punish us. But God doesn't want to do that because He loves us. God sent His dear Son Jesus who wanted to be punished for us. In this picture you can see Jesus being punished for your sins by dying there on the cross. That is how much Jesus loves you. He died for you.

John 19:16-24

Let's find out!

+ What are in Jesus' hands?
+ Why did Jesus let them kill Him?
+ Does Jesus love you?

This picture reminds me again of how You took my punishment, Lord Jesus. Thank You.

Jesus Is Dead

JESUS IS DEAD. His body is all wrapped up in a white cloth. His friends are putting His body into a great hole in the rock. Soon they will leave Him there all alone. They do not think they will ever see Jesus again. They will go away and leave Him here because He is dead. How sad they are! They do not know that soon He will become alive again and come out of the place where they are putting Him. Jesus is dead but God is going to bring Him back to life.

John 19:40-42

Let's find out!

✦ Where are they putting Jesus' body?
✦ Will His body stay there in the hole?

This is a picture of when You were dead. But You aren't dead anymore, Lord, and that makes me glad.

Jesus Is Alive Again

*T*HESE THREE WOMEN ARE JESUS' FRIENDS. They have come to His grave to put some sweet perfume on the clothes He was wrapped up in after He died. Then they would sadly go away and leave Jesus there and never see Him again. But what is happening? An angel is inside the grave where Jesus was. The angel tells them Jesus isn't there! Jesus is alive and has gone away! Jesus was dead, but God made Him alive again! Jesus said this would happen, but no one believed Him. Now His friends know that whatever Jesus says is always true. He says that He will make all His friends alive again after they are dead. He will take them up to heaven to be with Him always and always. Are you one of Jesus' friends? Aren't you glad that Jesus is alive?

Mark 16:1-8

Let's find out!

✦ Who are these women?
✦ What is the angel telling them?

What wonderful news! You are alive again, Lord Jesus, and someday You will take all Your friends to live with You in heaven. Thank You, thank You, thank You!

Jesus' Friends See Him

AT LAST SOME OF JESUS' FRIENDS ARE MEETING Him again. They are very surprised. They thought Jesus was dead. They didn't know that Jesus was alive again. They are walking along and they see somebody standing there, and it is Jesus! How surprised and happy they are. They know now that Jesus is God's Son and they fall down at His feet and pray to Him. Jesus is saying, "Don't be afraid. Go and tell My other friends to go to the place where I told them to meet Me."

Matthew 28:8-11

Let's find out!

✦ Who are these women talking to?
✦ Why are they surprised and happy?

The women are glad that You are alive again, Lord. I'm so glad, too.

346

Peter and John
Run to the Grave

*D*O YOU SEE THESE TWO MEN RUNNING as fast as they can? One of them is Peter and the other one is John. Peter is the older man and John is younger. Why are they running so fast? It is because the women have told them that Jesus is not in the grave but is alive again. Peter and John can hardly believe what the women have told them and they are going to see for themselves. They do not understand how Jesus could be alive and not in the hole in the rock. What an exciting morning this was when Jesus came back to life again!

John 20:1-5

Let's find out!

✦ Who are these two men?
✦ Where are they going?
✦ What will they find out?

Dear Lord, the women told these men that Jesus is alive. Thank You that somebody told me, too.

The Grave Is Empty

*P*ETER AND JOHN RAN right into the place where Jesus had been buried. In the picture you can see Peter inside, looking for Jesus. Is Jesus there? No, the cloth that was wrapped around Jesus is lying there, but Jesus has come out and gone away. He is alive again and isn't in the grave. Peter is surprised. John is surprised too. John is standing outside looking in. Finally they know that Jesus is not dead anymore.

John 20:6-10

Let's find out!

- Which man is Peter?
- Where is Jesus?

Dear Jesus, please help more and more people find out that You are alive, so now You can help them. Thank You.

Jesus Walks with Two Friends

*T*HREE MEN ARE WALKING ALONG A ROAD. Two of them are going to their home. When the third man came along and asked them why they were so sad they said it was because Jesus was dead. The third man began to tell them more about Jesus and why He had to die. He told them that Jesus died for their sins. The two men are asking this third man to come and eat with them. While they were eating, all of a sudden they realized that the third man was Jesus. They had been talking to Jesus and didn't know it! As soon as they knew this, suddenly Jesus disappeared and wasn't eating there with them anymore. He had gone away.

Luke 24:13-32

Let's find out!

✦ Who is the third man?

✦ What did he tell the other men?

Thank You, Jesus, that I can talk to You now even if I can't see You.

Jesus Shows His Hands and Feet

*T*HE DISCIPLES WERE TALKING TOGETHER when all of a sudden Jesus was standing there with them. He hadn't knocked or come in at the door. He was just there! He must have come right through the walls because Jesus can do anything. His disciples are scared but Jesus says, "Don't be afraid, I am Jesus." In this picture you can see Him showing His friends the holes in His hands and His feet, so that they will know that this is really their very own Jesus who was nailed to the big pieces of wood and died. Now He is alive again and they are seeing Him. Pretty soon He will eat some fish with them and some honey, so that they will know that He is really alive and is not just a ghost.

Luke 24:33-48

Let's find out!

✦ Who is the man talking to the disciples?

✦ Did He open the door and come in?

Thank You, Father God, that the same Jesus who died on the cross is alive again.

Jesus Goes Back to Heaven

ONE DAY WHILE JESUS WAS TALKING with His disciples out on a hill, all of a sudden He began to go up into the air. Do you see the cloud there above Him? Jesus went into the cloud and they will not see Him anymore. Do you know where He is going? He is going to heaven to live again with God His Father. When Jesus had gone away, two angels came and talked with Jesus' friends and told them that Jesus will come back again someday. Someday Jesus is going to come and take all His friends to Heaven. Are you one of Jesus' friends?

Acts 1:9-11

Let's find out!

✦ Where is Jesus going?

✦ Will He come back again?

Thank You, Jesus, that someday You'll come back and I'll get to see You.

The Holy Spirit Comes

ONE DAY WHILE JESUS' FRIENDS WERE PRAYING together, there came a noise that sounded like a big wind coming from the sky, and the noise was all around them in the house, although they couldn't feel any wind. Do you see what is on the people's heads? It looks like tongues made of fire on each of them. Why is this happening? It is because God the Holy Spirit is coming down upon these people. After a while the tongues of fire will go away but the Holy Spirit will stay in their hearts. The Holy Spirit will help them and tell them many things and make them very strong. Jesus sent the Holy Spirit to comfort and help them.

Acts 2:1-3

Let's find out!

✦ What is on the people's heads?

✦ Who is coming into these people?

✦ Who sent the Holy Spirit to them?

Lord Jesus, thank You that You, and God the Father, and God the Holy Spirit want to live in me. Yes, please come live inside me.

Peter Preaches about Jesus

*P*ETER IS TALKING TO ALL of these other people who don't know about Jesus yet. He is telling them that Jesus wants to be their friend and their Savior. They have come from many countries where the people have their own languages. But Peter and the other Christians are talking to them in their own languages. God is helping Peter and the other disciples to talk in whatever language they need to tell people about Jesus. When these people hear about Jesus dying for them they are sad and ask what they should do. Peter tells them to believe in the Lord Jesus, and many of them did.

Acts 2:4-8, 14-21

Let's find out!

+ What is Peter telling these people?
+ Do they decide to love Jesus?

Father God, please send more people to tell men and woman and boys and girls everywhere about Jesus.

A Lame Man Walks

*P*ETER AND JOHN have come to God's house to pray. A man is sitting there who can't walk. Something is the matter with his legs. He was that way when he was a tiny baby and he has never been able to walk. That is why he is sitting there near God's house asking people to give him money to buy food. When he sees Peter and John he asks them to give him some money. Peter said he didn't have any, but he could give him something else that was a lot better. He said, "Get up and walk. Jesus will make you well." In the picture you can see the man beginning to get up. He will walk and run. He will give thanks to God.

Acts 3:1-11

Let's find out!

+ Could this man walk before Peter talked to him?

+ Where is Jesus?

+ Did Jesus help Peter make the man walk?

Dear Lord, thank You for using Peter and John to heal this man. I'm thankful, too, for all the good things You do for me.

Peter and John Will Obey God

PETER IS TALKING TO THE BAD MEN who killed Jesus. They don't like Peter and would like to kill him. They are angry because Peter said it was the power of Jesus that made the man walk, who was sitting on the steps of God's house. In the picture you can see the man standing there with Peter. When Peter tells them that Jesus made the man well again, they tell Peter not to talk about Jesus anymore. But Peter isn't obeying them. Peter obeys God, but not these men, so he will keep on telling how kind and wonderful Jesus is.

Acts 4:5-21

Let's find out!

✦ Do the bad people want Peter to talk about Jesus?

✦ Will Peter stop talking about Jesus?

Help me, Father God, to do what's right, even if some people laugh at me and want me to do things that are wrong.

364

Ananias Lies to God

*T*HE MAN LYING DOWN ON THE FLOOR IS DEAD. The man standing up is Peter. Peter was sitting there and the man came in and told him a lie. As soon as he told the lie he suddenly fell down and died. God punished him because he told a lie. Soon the people will carry him outside and make a hole in the ground and put him in it and cover him up.

Acts 5:1-11

Let's find out!

✦ Why is the man there on the floor?
✦ Did he tell a lie to God?

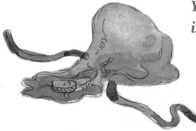

You want Your people to say only what is true, Lord. Help me never to tell lies.

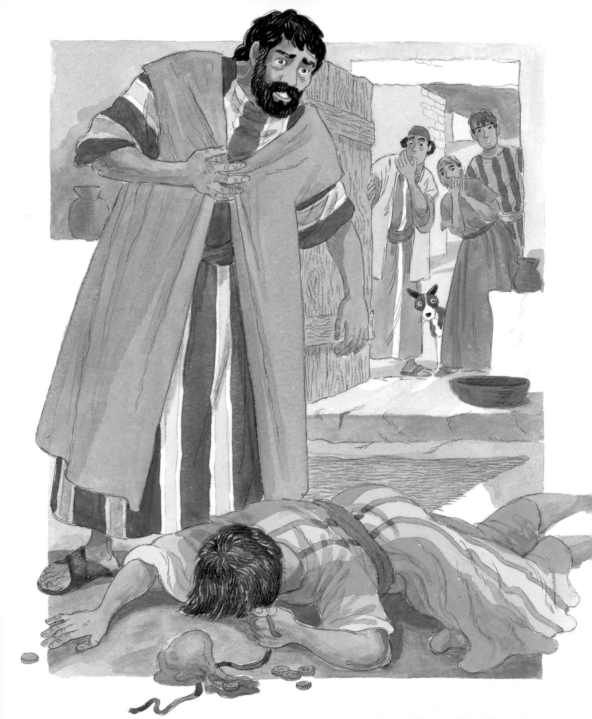

God's Angel Helps Peter

PETER IS IN JAIL. The people who killed Jesus have put him there. The doors and windows are all locked so that he can't get out. He has been there all night. Here in this picture you can see Peter lying there in jail when all of a sudden an angel comes. The angel is waking Peter up and telling him to come with him. The angel will unlock the doors of the jail. The angel doesn't have a key but he will open the doors anyway. When he is safely out he will tell Peter to go and tell more people about Jesus. God sent His angel to help Peter.

Acts 12:1-17

Let's find out!

✦ Does the angel have a key to the door?

✦ What did the angel tell Peter to do?

Father God, I'm glad that sometimes You send Your angels to help me even if I can't see them.

Stephen Goes to Heaven

OH, WHAT IS HAPPENING TO THIS MAN? He is kneeling down and praying while the bad men are killing him with big stones. Is he crying? No. He is praying and asking God not to hurt these men even though they are hurting him. His name is Stephen. These men are angry because Stephen told them about Jesus. They didn't want to hear about Jesus and so they decided to kill Stephen. Stephen is happy because he sees Jesus up there in heaven. In a little while he will go there and be with Jesus.

Acts 6:8-15; 7:54-60

Let's find out!

✦ What is the man's name?
✦ Why are these men throwing big stones at him?

Dear Lord, please help all the people in other countries who are in jail because they tell others about Jesus, and that He can forgive their sins.

370

Philip Explains God's Book

THE MAN SITTING IN THE CHARIOT and reading the Book wants to know more about God. He is reading part of the Bible. He has stopped the horses and is talking to Philip. The Holy Spirit told Philip to run over to the chariot and start talking to the man. He is telling the man what the Bible means. He is telling him about Jesus. Soon the man sitting in the chariot will be a Christian.

Acts 8:26-40

Let's find out!

✦ What is the man's name who is standing there?

✦ Who is he talking about?

✦ Will the other man become a Christian?

Father God, thank You so much for Your Book, the Bible. If there wasn't a Bible, we wouldn't know about Jesus.

Paul Hurts God's People

*T*HIS MAN'S NAME IS PAUL. He doesn't like
Christians. He would like to kill all of them or put
them in jail. He is walking down the road trying to find
some Christians to hurt. He thinks that all Christians are
bad. He does not know that Jesus is God's Son. Paul thinks
God wants him to hurt Christians. But soon Jesus will
speak to Paul from heaven and tell him not to hurt God's
people. Then Paul will stop hurting them and spend his
life helping them.

Acts 9:1, 2

Let's find out!

✦ What is this man's name?

✦ Why does he hurt the Christians?

*Dear Lord, please keep Your people safe
today from others who want to hurt
them.*

374

Paul Hears Jesus' Voice

*H*ERE IS ANOTHER PICTURE OF PAUL. While he was walking down the road all of a sudden God started talking to him from heaven. He is telling Paul not to hurt the Christians anymore. He is saying, "Paul, you too must become one of My friends. I am Jesus, and you must stop hurting Me and you must leave My people alone." Paul is very surprised and afraid, and is asking Jesus what He wants him to do. Jesus tells him, and now Paul will always do whatever Jesus says.

Acts 9:3-19

Let's find out!

✦ Who is talking to Paul?
✦ Does Paul decide to love Jesus?

Thank You, Lord, that You can change even people like Paul so that they will love You. I'm glad.

376

Friends Help Paul Get Away

*W*HO IS THIS MAN IN THE BASKET? It is Paul. His friends are helping him to get away. Paul has been telling everyone about his new Friend Jesus and how much he loves Him. Paul doesn't hurt God's children anymore. The people who don't like Paul try to catch him and kill him, so his friends are helping him to run away. Paul is God's friend now and he loves Jesus.

Acts 9:22-28

Let's find out!

✦ Who is the man in the basket?
✦ Why is he running away?

Thank You, Lord, for giving Paul good friends to help him. Please give me good friends, too.

Paul and Silas Are in Jail

*P*AUL AND SILAS ARE IN JAIL, but they don't care because they know that God loves them. They have been singing in jail. They have been whipped, and now they are chained to the wall. All of a sudden a great earthquake shakes the jail and all of the doors swing open and the chains fall off their hands and feet so that they can run away. But they are not trying to run away. They are staying there and talking to the man who is supposed to keep them in jail. He is kneeling there asking them what to do. They are telling him to believe on Jesus and he will be saved.

Acts 16:22-34

Let's find out!

✦ Where are Paul and Silas?

✦ Who are they talking to?

✦ What did they tell the man to do?

Thank You that the jailer asked Peter and John how to have his sins forgiven.

Paul Is Safe in the Storm

*P*AUL IS ON A BOAT and there is a great storm. Do you see the waves and how the ship is sinking? But God took care of Paul and all the people who were with him and none of them were hurt. They came through the water and got to the shore all right. Paul is standing there telling God, "Thank You," for taking care of them. God loves Paul, and God loves you.

Acts 27:14-44

Let's find out!

✦ Did the ship sink?

✦ Were the people saved?

✦ Does God love you?

You do love me, Lord, and You take care of me. Thank You for saving Paul from the storm, and for loving me.